To Gerrie
Best Regards

WHO DYED MY HAIR
WHITE IN THE NIGHT?

Reflections of a Perennial Child

Polly Rogers Brown

Polly Rogers Brown

ISBN: 1539382877
ISBN 13: 9781539382874
Library of Congress Control Number: 2016916743
CreateSpace Independent Publishing Platform
North Charleston, South Carolina

FORWARD AND ACKNOWLEDGEMENTS
BY POLLY ROGERS BROWN

Thanks to my family for encouraging me to put my stories in a book. Their patient listening and appreciation over the years has given me the courage to leap into an unknown world and pretend to be a writer. Thanks to my patient husband Wayne who listened and laughed at the right times and gave me the will to keep going. Thanks to my friend Mary who lovingly nagged me into publishing my first book. Thanks to Ana, Lydia, and Jordan, my three granddaughters, for excusing me for not mentioning them in my stories even though their four brothers are, and who will have equal time in my next book.

CHAPTER 1

EARLY SCHOOL DAYS

I look back on my elementary education with warmth and amusement. Those eight years I spent in LaFevre School were rich in sound and sight and taste and smell – an education for the senses as well as for the mind.

The families who sent their children to LaFevre generally fell into one of two categories: either they were old stock whose parents and grandparents had lived in the same house before them, or they were the transient poor who came and went, using the school as a temporary shelter for their ragged children before they could or had to move on.

Each year brought a new crop of culls and runts and misfits. I remember little boys and girls in absurd clothes, crusty gray ankles showing above shoes with no laces, carrying with them the smell of poverty and neglect.

They often had no lunch pails to line up with ours on the shelf above the coat hooks, and they eyed our food at lunch time with a mixture of lust and reverence. We often gave them some of our food, motivated by the echoes of our mothers' admonishments about sharing in the back of our minds, but also by a kind of curiosity as we watched them fall upon our gifts with a fervor that both intrigued and frightened us.

We never learned much about each other, and they disappeared after a few weeks or months, leaving little behind and moving on to less.

But most of us came from families whose names and addresses were fixtures in the community. The Welches and Davenports and Rogerses and Kerns and Titsworths and Kowitzes and Rinesses and Baxters sent their children with regularity, confident that whatever education was necessary in life would be doled out by the teachers they hired at the yearly school board meeting in early summer.

Often times were hard and choices were few, and the community had to take what they could get. The teachers they hired were a unique lot, some proficient and capable, some listless and incompetent.

There was Bell Watson, ancient and inept, who wet her pants daily and rinsed them in the enamel washbasin and hung them to dry on the towering furnace in the back of the single room. We'd stand on each other's shoulders and peer through the windows to catch her rinsing her underwear at lunch time after she'd locked us outside.

Then Miss Drexel marshalled me through two years, rigid and austere, her love for her students bound up tightly behind her serge suit and corset.

Miss Beachwell followed, muddling through two years. Plump and freckled and young, she giggled and primped and painted her lips orange with liquid lipstick in a tiny glass bottle. She fell in love with a young man from the neighborhood, and we spent long recesses in autumn while they courted coyly in his rusty Ford beside the woodshed.

Finally Mrs. Schanskey marched in and restored order for the remainder of my elementary years. She was dully Germanic, and we learned the virtues of straight lines and uniformity and silence. She was solid and plain and uncomplicated, and she unknowingly fostered in me a passion to be special, a strong need to be unique, a resolve never to be like her.

⚒

The children who attended LaFevre school were often far more entertaining than the subject matter we studied. Take the four Sage boys. They lived just north of the school in a two-room shack that sat in weeds and brush, its front door rarely closed, ragged curtains fluttering from open windows.

Their father Bert rarely intruded into either their lives or ours because he worked in a factory in Flint and was home very little. On Sunday afternoon he walked seven miles to Millington to catch a ride, and he returned home after work on Friday.

We usually saw him only twice during the school year - once on Halloween and once on Valentine's Day. On these special days Bert would bring pop to school, a wonderful and unexpected luxury. He lugged in the low wooden boxes with "Nehi" printed on the sides, wooden dividers check-rowing the bottles of jewel-like colors. Bright green, purple, red, orange - I always picked red. It tasted of magical fruit and the beautiful claret dazzled me. I loved the fiery burn of the liquid as it slid down my throat, making me belch little cascades of soda bubbles that tickled my nose. It was with a kind of reverence that I handled the bottle, like the way I lifted and replaced the tiny communion glasses at church.

We never would have accepted any gifts from Bert other than those safely sealed in glass. The oily sheen of his filthy pants and the stiff, crusty hairs that grew out of his ears spoiled our appetites for anything which he might have had a personal hand in preparing.

Bert was wiry and small, and his skin had the unhealthy pallor of one who has no one about to make him eat his vegetables. His boys were dingy and unkempt, and their lunches were the only things about them that gave me cause for envy. My lunch sack yielded food which I looked upon with scorn for its commonness: tomato sandwiches on homemade bread, slices of cold pot roast, apples from the orchard, dill pickles from the crock in the basement, homemade pineapple-raisin cake whose frosting stuck to the waxed paper in which it was wrapped.

The Sage boys, however, had lunches of wonderful food that came from a section of the grocery store in which my parents never shopped. They had fine white bread with round slices of bologna dotted with sliced olives, and perfect little chocolate cupcakes in cellophane with white frosting crosses on their tops. They had starchy little pies in pretty wrappers, and they were filled with clear red cherry juice that squeezed out when they took a bite. They had wonderful cookies in the shape of little Dutch windmills, and they had candy bars with names on the wrappers like Whiz and Zagnut and Baby Ruth.

I longed to bring lunches to school like theirs, foods in clear paper that crackled when you picked it up, foods that had been bought in a store, not made on the wood range or brought up from the basement.

I was a precocious child who had the misconception that she was, and always had been, an adult. When I was three I learned to read. It was a very unremarkable act which created little flurry in my family, all avid readers themselves, so I had no reason to be impressed with the accomplishment myself. More impressive to me was my skill at passing long afternoon hours of nap time bur-rowed under the quilt with a book and a flashlight, read-ing my older sisters' novels of passion and intrigue. My ability to fake the look of a child just awakened from an afternoon nap and to completely fool my mother gave me great satisfaction.

When I began school I was surprised by the simple and childish books I was given to read. They were stories that only a ninny would like; I craved adventure, romance, and action. The reading books of the upper grades were still not completely to my liking, but at least they were filled with people who had modest adventures to which they were able to respond with more than "Oh, oh, funny, funny Spot."

When Miss Drexel realized that I was sneaking reading books into my desk that were grades above me, she wisely decided to give me a job that was to our mutual benefit. She put me in charge of all reading classes, filling me with a wonderful sense of importance, and easing her own burden of teaching all subjects to eight grades.

Each day as the reading classes were called to the front of the room I would stand before their semicircle of stocky little oak chairs and listen to them read aloud. They didn't seem to resent my corrections, probably looking at me as such an oddity that they had no reason to feel threatened.

One day in early spring I stood, as usual, before the eighth-grade class as they read aloud about an explorer on the brink of disaster, having just had his entire food supply devoured by a pack of marauding wolves who now eyed him hungrily. My thoughts were not on the explorer and his plight but on my own, having failed to visit the outhouse at recess, and realizing that I was approaching a real crisis as a result. I faced two unthinkable choices - asking the teacher if I might be excused to go to the outhouse, thereby humiliating myself in the eyes of the entire school, or running the risk of wetting my pants, a possibility growing more probable by the minute.

I stood frozen in emotional and physical agony. I hoped for a miracle, for my fairy godmother to appear, anything to rescue me from impending doom. I waited in vain. Finally the inevitable and the unspeakable happened. I felt a kind of desperate relief as I watched a puddle gather at my feet. It began to follow the center grain of one of the rough and uneven floorboards. It lengthened into a tiny river which ran toward the eighth graders who sat transfixed, staring in disbelief. Before the river reached their feet it was mercifully diverted by a small knot hole into which it ran, disappearing beneath the floorboards.

My humiliation was complete. No other indignity could have hurt me further. Laughter, leering faces, pointing fingers, shouts of derision - none of these could have touched me. I was numb with shock, dazed and unaware of anything around me.

The hurried dismissal by Miss Drexel, the rapid clearing of the building for an early lunch, the solace of kind hands and soothing words was lost on me. I was beyond comfort and consolation. My life was over. I would never be seen in public again.

━◁┼▷━

An important highlight in our school year was the occasional visit by Earnestine Kern. "Visit" really doesn't do justice to these encounters; "assaults" would be more accurate. Mrs. Kern would sweep down on us, generally to attack the teacher, student body, in fact, most of humanity for misusing one of her three boys.

One of us might have offended Norman, tall, lanky, with a bony, hooked nose that invited derision. Or perhaps someone had provoked Albert into one of his violent fits of rage, the effects of which rendered him relatively weak and often led to his sulking behind a black eye or a split lip. Or perhaps someone had picked on Duane, humiliating him into shedding public tears, thus compromising his budding manhood. Whatever the reason, Mrs. Kern did not take kindly to her boys being picked on, and, like an old setting hen whose feathers had been ruffled, she would swoop down, squawking and all aflutter.

Her very knock at the door demanded instant attention. She started rapping sharply and didn't stop until Mrs. Shanskey opened the door. By this time she had a good head of steam up and she'd begin her attack.

She usually started with a general condemnation of society at large, gradually narrowing it down to the educational system in general, then finally coming to rest on LaFevre School, most specifically Mrs. Shanskey, her incompetence, stupidity, and penchant for promoting environments in which the Kern boys were subject to abuse.

As her voice rose by octaves and decibels, her color deepened. Her orange hair which coiled into stiff curls that flared back in a magnificent upsweep threatened to come unlacquered and clatter to the floor in individual ringlets as she shook her head and stamped her feet. Her tight little bosom quivered dangerously as she built up steam.

We sat frozen in our seats, loving the peril our teacher faced, hoping the fight would continue, feeling the wondrous clutch of terror at our hearts as Mrs. Kern raged on.

Finally exhaustion set in and she began to wind down. The tirade became repetitious, and each new verbal attack had a ring of familiarity. The two adversaries gradually drew back, too tired to maintain the toe-to-toe posture much longer. Mrs. Kern felt the need to reiterate a few of her stronger points, but with less venom than before, and Mrs. Shanskey didn't fend off the barbs with quite as much vigor. The fight was over.

We collectively relaxed and began breathing normally again. The fun was over until Mrs. Kern's next visit.

I was introduced to the intricate ritual of necking in the entryway of my one-room school in the spring of my sixth grade. I was not entirely naïve – I had been kissed before, but only in quick pecks delivered furtively and followed by mutual embarrassment as we both pretended it had all been a silly error. But standing in the entryway watching Norman Kern and Alicia Titsworth, I knew beyond a doubt that what I was seeing was the deliberate movements of two people who were clearly enjoying themselves.

They were cuddled together on the wooden bench under the coat hooks, and Alicia's green plaid coat was draped over them like a tent. Norman's long, bony arms undulated around her, clutching alternately at her and the coat which kept slipping off their heads and dropping to the bench. Their faces were flushed and moist, and their eyes had a peculiar glassy look. Even though I stood clearly in their line of vision, I seemed to be quite invisible to them, their eyes not quite focusing on the things around them.

They breathed as if they were in pain or had just run to the brink of exhaustion. Short gasps were followed by long sighs, then all breathing would stop until they were forced to take in quick gulps of air.

Norman seemed unable to decide whether he preferred his lips to be puckered on hers or pursed in the hollow of her neck, and each time he changed locations he had trouble relocating his large, bony nose which intruded and hampered his progress.

Alicia, who had never particularly liked Norman in the past, was suddenly quite enthralled with his back and his hair. One arm twined behind him and rubbed his sharp shoulder blades while the other circled his neck, alternately smoothing then ruffling his sandy hair.

They both looked quite disheveled, their clothes rumpled and askew. Alicia's white blouse began to come untucked from her skirt band, and Nelson's pant legs crept up above his socks, showing white, hairless calves.

I knew that what I was watching would best be left unmentioned when I went home. I had a feeling my mother would neither share my fascination with these actions nor be interested in a lengthy discussion of their implications. It would be best to wait until my friend Wanda Davenport and I could talk in private; then we would sort out the truth about this thing called necking.

CHAPTER 2

THE DIPPER

"Fred, when you do the trading this week, look for a little dipper, will you? I need it for canning."

Dad looked across the kitchen table with as much interest as he could muster. His mind was somewhere in the back forty, judging the height of the alfalfa and calculating the drying time after mowing.

"Did you hear me? I need a dipper."

"A dipper," Dad murmured.

"One to use for canning. About two or three cups. And get one with a nice long handle so I don't burn myself when I ladle tomatoes into jars."

"Write it down on the list," Dad said. The list was a collection of things Mother needed to feed and tend to her six children for the upcoming week.

On Saturday morning Dad would take it from Mother, read it silently, fold it, and place it in the top pocket of his bibbed overalls. Later he would take it out and place each item listed there in the metal cart as he pushed it down the narrow aisles of Cobbs' General Store in Millington.

That's how I imagine the dipper came to belong with the canning supplies in my parents' wooden corner cupboard. During each canning season Mother would use it to ladle fruits and vegetables into scalded Mason jars to be processed and stored for the long winter ahead.

It was put to unusual and unexpected use when I was about four years old. Our neighbor, Mary Welch, had married a handsome young man and they had just returned from their honeymoon. As was the custom in the early 1940's, the church planned a chivaree to welcome them home. A chivaree was a deliciously naughty gathering after midnight beneath the bedroom window of the newlyweds. The revelers would sneak up silently, then on a given signal create a deafening clamor with noisemakers – shotguns, whistles, drums, bells – anything to wrest the inhabitants from sleep, wide-eyed with terror.

My noisemaker was Mother's aluminum dipper, turned upside down in one hand, and a large wooden spoon in the other. At the given signal I pounded with all my might, the noise drowned out the by the more sophisticated instruments of clamor around me. Lights came on in the bedroom and tousled heads appeared in the window, and we shrieked with laughter and yelled our congratulations and best wishes to the new couple.

Later on as we ambled back to our cars, still laughing and reveling in the chaos we had created, I noticed Mother's dipper and my heart sank. I had beaten the bottom with such enthusiasm that I had caved it in and dented it beyond repair. With dread and sorrow I showed it to Mother when we returned home. Surprisingly, she was not upset at all. She merely said, "It was worth it. Don't worry, Sweetie, Dad will fix it."

The next morning the dipper disappeared with Dad and reappeared a bit later with its bottom dimpled and dented, but remarkably flat and still usable.

For years the dipper served Mother well at canning time. I had little interest in it, and as I grew up I forgot, in fact, that it existed.

Then fifty years later as the Rogers' children stood sadly in the old farmhouse facing the solemn duty of dividing up our parents' worldly goods, someone began to empty the old kitchen cupboard. There was the dipper, still dented and dimpled, and something in me yearned to take it home and put it with my own canning supplies.

And there it is today. I still ladle steaming tomatoes and apple sauce and grape juice into scalded Mason jars to be processed and stored for the long winter ahead.

CHAPTER 3

GETTING RICH AND OTHER
UNSUCCESSFUL VENTURES

No one in my family ever had much money. Mother had a few coins and an occasional dollar bill in her handbag, and Dad kept his small stash folded and tucked away in his billfold, or "purse" as we all called it, which was kept in the top drawer of the dresser in his bedroom under a stack of yellowed envelopes and next to a fascinating collection of things that had no useful purpose but were such fun to look at.

My wealth was contained in a small, cylindrical, silver-colored dime bank with a slot in the top and a scale from zero to five dollars next to a vertical opening that let me glimpse the glorious and growing stack of dimes that fell into my possession.

Sometimes I found coins in the dirt parking lot at church, or in the graveled parking area next to Cobb's General Store in Millington. Sometimes Dad would give me a dollar to spend at the dime store where I dawdled as he bought the week's groceries next door at Cobb's. I would hand him the change when we were on our way home, but usually he just waved it away and told me to put it back in my pocket. How I loved those words, and the quiet man whose own store of wealth was so meager but who read the shy heart of his freckled six-year-old daughter sitting next to him in the rusty '38 Chevy. Those coins were changed into dimes, and they were dropped, one by one, in the slot of my dime bank.

My financial portfolio remained virtually unchanged until I was twelve and the neighbors hired me on rare occasions to babysit their three small children while they went out for the evening. They lived two miles away in a pleasant two-story farm house on the edge of a swamp. Their children were amiable and easily entertained, and my job was not difficult.

There were, however, drawbacks. The parents would pick me up around seven in the evening and tell me they would be home by midnight. About eleven I would begin pacing through the house, watching the dirt road in both directions, yearning to see headlights headed my way. The rare car that approached would not slow down but would speed by in a cloud of dust that settled on my sinking heart. This continued until my employers' return, which was never by midnight, but more likely 1:30 or later. They would breeze in smelling of smoky worldliness, never seeming to notice that they had stayed out so late.

It wasn't just the duration of my tour of duty that troubled me. My cowardly heart pounded madly through most of the evening and my mind conjured up doom and disaster. For one thing, the doors had no locks that worked. Any crazed maniac hiding in the nearby swamp could walk in on me and that would be that for my hopes of seeing another day. The curtains at the windows could not be closed to keep me concealed from such marauders that gathered in the dark. The two dogs in the yard added to my terror by circling the house growling and barking frantically through most of the evening, undoubtedly trying to warn me of the menace that lurked behind the trees waiting for the right moment to burst in and nab me.

When the parents finally arrived I would be limp with relief, answering their questions about how the children had behaved and if I had had any problems during the evening. I could not bring myself to mention the desperate peril I had been in for the last six hours, especially since they seemed so comfortable with the dangerous environment in which they lived.

Then when the father would drive me home I would sit stiffly next to him hoping that he would sense the mental anguish he had caused me and pay me commensurately, perhaps fifty cents an hour, which would add up to at least three dollars. After he stopped at my back door he would hand me my pay which I would accept with a polite murmur, hurrying into my house, grateful that the evening was over. I would examine the pay folded in my hand, despairing to find a one-dollar bill and a few quarters, half of what I thought I had earned.

The lean years continued throughout most of my early adolescence. Most of the other neighbors were as poor as my family, and no one was interested in hiring a girl to do work their own children could do for free.

The exception in this bleak financial picture was a single bright spot every summer around late June. Our local one-room school was given a thorough cleaning before the new year began, and the job was farmed out at the local school board meeting which I attended with my family.

I would sit as quietly as possible while my father, the president of the school board, attended to the necessities of providing for the needs of the upcoming year. A modest budget allowed for minimal supplies, the salary of a teacher who would manage kindergarten through eighth grade, and an allotment for the light bill and wood for the furnace in the back of the room.

Then came the part which made my heart race - the hiring of a person to clean the school.

Each applicant was asked to submit a dollar figure and his name on a slip of paper to be considered for the job.

As I feigned nonchalance and pondered my price, I would watch Mrs. Kern, my arch rival for the job. She fidgeted and dawdled, covertly filling out her slip of paper and adding it to the small pile in front of my father.

She was easy to read. Any situation with the least amount of stress caused her to flush a deep red that clashed with the flamboyant orange curls lacquered high on her head. She would avoid any eye contact with me, probably hoping that ignoring me would give me a false sense of security and I would give in to greed and write down a number higher than hers. When she had submitted her bid I would casually add my slip of paper to the small pile on the teacher's desk.

After a brief consultation was held between Father and the treasurer, the winning bid was announced and the job was awarded to the person willing to work for the least amount of money. I always got the job. I was young and my fiscal awareness was underdeveloped. The three days of hard work ahead - washing the tall windows on the inside and out, scrubbing each wooden desk with a brush and soap and water, sweeping and dusting the accumulated residue of last year's messy and careless students - this misery paled in comparison to the prospect of twenty-five dollars of my very own, to be spent at Robert Hall discount clothing store in Saginaw on next year's school clothes.

This was heady success, indeed. It surpassed the satisfaction I would feel ten years later when I cashed my first paycheck as an English teacher at Mayville High School. This cleaning job signaled my entry into the world of commerce and financial security. I was a working woman who had competed with a grown-up neighbor and vanquished her soundly. Life was good.

CHAPTER 4

UNTRUSTWORTHY VEHICLES I HAVE KNOWN

Vehicles and I have an uneasy history. From my earliest memory involving a rusty tricycle that I fought in vain to conquer to the present in which sleek, modern vehicles sulk in the driveway dribbling puddles of iridescent coolant, a fleet of machines with bad attitudes fill the junkyard of my mind.

As a child I never expected much in the line of dependable transportation. Everyone I knew drove rusty hulks that backfired and belched smoke and periodically shot geysers of steam from over-heated radiators. It was common to drive past neighbors whose back yards held old Hudsons and Nashes resting on cement blocks, their greasy motors dangling from chain falls which hung askew from sturdy tree limbs above. The men of the family leaned on the front fenders, their heads under the open hoods, pondering the mysteries of the internal combustion engine.

My earliest memory of personal transportation was a tricycle handed down from an older sister. My legs were too short to reach the pedals, so I developed a system in which I lurched from side to side, shifting my weight to touch one pedal at a time. The seat had come partly unfastened from the frame, and it tended to pitch me off into the yellow sand of our driveway unexpectedly. The front wheel was bent and rubbed against the fender, adding to my difficulty in forward motion. All in all, cycling at this stage of my life was far less than I had hoped for.

My second encounter with an unruly bike occurred when I was ten years old and was spending the afternoon with Glenadine Griffen. She lived at the highest of a series of steep hills, and the gravel road that passed her house was precarious in summer and impassable in winter. We grew tired of her back yard swing and were looking for new diversions. The garage door was open and our eyes fell upon two bicycles in the shadows. One was hers, a girl's bike with shiny chrome fenders, the other her six-foot brother's, a stripped-down speed demon with handle bars that curled under like a mountain goat's horns.

Glenadine pushed her bike out into the sunlight and I followed with her brother's. We thought it might be fun to coast down the hill that began at the end of her driveway and ended a quarter of a mile below. I was somewhat troubled by the size of my bike, its seat level with my shoulders and the distance between the pedals and the cross bar above several inches greater than my inseam. I propped it against the mailbox and climbed up, perching precariously on the racing seat that was definitely not built for comfort. I pushed off, following Glenadine down the gravel track.

As I gathered speed I became aware that it might be advantageous if I were to have my feet on the pedals in case it became necessary to apply the brakes. It quickly became clear that braking was necessary. The bike shot down the steep incline, flinging gravel stones behind it as I clung to the handlebars, hunched forward, legs straining downward to touch the pedals which were cycling madly just beyond my reach. I began to swerve and careen dangerously close to the brush-lined ditch to my right. I had no choice. I shifted my weight to one leg and hiked up the other to clear the cross bar and came down hard on the pedal. As my luck would have it, I caught the pedal in the back swing, activated the brake, and in a flurry of gravel and dust I and the bike were catapulted into the ditch. I lay still, dazed and unsure that I would ever walk again, the overturned bike on top of me, its wheels still turning at a frantic pace.

After a suitable recuperation period, I pushed the bike back up the hill and left if in the garage where I had found it. Glenadine and I decided to pursue less vigorous diversions for the rest of the afternoon, among which were picking small pieces of gravel out of my skinned kneecaps.

Another mechanical challenge from my early years was the old farm stake bed truck. It was a monster with enormous front fenders, a rust-riddled grill that clung to the hood, and a bumper that sagged at one end, giving the front end the look of a spent giant with a wry grimace of defeat.

We used the truck to haul hay in summertime, and I, being too small to fork the loose hay into place on the back, was the appointed driver. Dad would hook the tongue of the hay loader to the back of the truck and he and my brother Bill would climb up on the wooden bed and lean against the cab, their forks jabbed into the wood floor for balance. I'd hear Dad say "OK, Polly, let 'er out nice and easy."

The dreaded moment was upon me. I sat perched on the front of the seat, legs dangling above the gaping holes in the rusted floor, peering through the steering wheel that was several inches higher than my head. Stretching my left leg as far as I could, I pushed the clutch pedal to the floor and with my right hand wrenched the floor shift into creeper. Then I groped with my right foot for the gas pedal which was little more than a metal rod emerging from the floor, the foot-shaped covering having disappeared years earlier.

Then I tried my best to simultaneously let out the clutch with one leg and push down on the gas with the other. The old truck would lurch and wheeze forward and I would hear the scrabble of work boots as Dad and Bill pitched about behind me.

Once in motion, we were a curious sight. A sputtering old truck straddling a windrow of hay, two men clinging to the back of the cab, and a hay loader rattling behind, its metal teeth scooping up the hay and moving it up the cradle that loomed over the back of the truck, all controlled by a driver who peeped through the steering wheel, scarcely tall enough to see through the bottom of the windshield.

Once safely in motion, the truck nearly drove itself. It idled in creeper, barely moving along, and I could sit back on the seat and concentrate on keeping the truck astraddle the long rows of hay that Bill had raked earlier.

The heat rose in waves from the hood of the truck, and the spicy scent of new hay filled the cab. Sometimes I'd grow drowsy from the heat, and Dad's voice with jerk me back to the present when I strayed off the windrow. I would wrench the wheel and move back to the long row of hay, leaving behind a short stretch to be picked up the next time around the field.

With great relief I would eventually hear Dad yell "Wup, Polly," and I'd shift into neutral and stop, sliding over and waiting for the two men to climb down from the load, unhitch the hay loader, and climb into the cab. Dad would drive to the barn and back the truck into the center. Then we'd head to the house for a cold drink before we unloaded the hay and returned to the field for another load.

The old truck saw us through many haying seasons during which I slowly inched my way upward until I could see over the steering wheel. Then one hot day in mid-July fate stepped in and the old relic breathed its last. Dad had stopped by the back porch to add a gallon of water to the radiator, and he grabbed the customary amber gallon jug that had once contained Roman Cleanser Bleach. He poured the contents into the radiator and a strange chemical smell and a cloud of steam arose from the opening. Dad sniffed the jug and a rare expletive bubbled up and singed my ears; the jug had, in actuality, contained bleach. It was washday Monday and Mother had set it there for safe-keeping rather than leave it inside the back door where one of us might have stumbled over it and created a mess. We took the rest of the day off while Dad recovered his composure and planned for his next farm truck.

The only other vehicle that transported the six Rogers' children and their parents was generally a very old, very rusty Chevrolet. Dad would bring a slightly updated relic home from the Chevy dealership in Millington after the current one had groaned and rattled its last mile and was beyond resuscitation. Generally the replacement had fewer holes in the floorboards, the pedals and gear shift were securely attached, and the windows actually rolled up and down when the handles were rotated. An unexpected touch of luxury sometimes came in the form of cloth seats, rather than stiff vinyl ones that stuck to your bare legs on hot summer days and nearly peeled the skin off when you stood up.

I learned to drive such a car when I was thirteen. I was proficient at steering a hay truck or driving the John Deere B around a corn field, but actually steering a real car down a public road with ditches on both sides while other cars sailed toward you could be disconcerting. Especially with my mother in the front seat next to me. This became painfully clear to me on my first solo trip home from church one Sunday evening.

I was the fourth child to be initiated into the art of driving and my mother was showing definite signs of wear from the three siblings who had preceded me in the driver's seat. Not only was her patience wearing thin, but her confidence in teenage drivers had been eroded by several hair-raising episodes which she related to me about my older siblings and their reckless driving habits.

I reassured her that I would be careful and follow all her instructions, and she relaxed a bit and gave me a weak smile. Then she launched into a long list of mechanical skills I would have to practice, most of which I had mastered by the age of nine, sitting behind the wheel of the old hay truck. I knew better than to correct her misconceptions, having learned that once she started such instructions she had the uncontrollable need to finish the list down to the last minute detail.

At last we were ready. I pushed the clutch in and shifted into first. I stepped on the gas and just as I was ready to ease the clutch out Mother shrieked something about another car pulling out in my path. I shot backward in the seat and the car leaped forward and mercifully stalled before we made contact. I looked at Mother who was clutching the door handle and leaning into the window with a vacant look of horror in her eyes. I would soon come to recognize that look every time I made even the tiniest of driving errors.

When she had composed herself I slowly nosed the old car toward the road. I turned right onto the sand two-track and began the climb up the steep hill just south of the church. I was still in first gear, and half way up the hill Mother suggested I shift into second. I had a momentary lapse in which I forgot what that meant and I looked down to see where my feet were and to try and remember what to do with them.

The second shriek from Mother jerked my attention back to the road ahead of me, and I saw a rusty pickup breaking over the hill and heading straight toward me. As Mother clutched her door handle with one hand and her throat with the other, I wrenched the wheel and drove up the bank on the wrong side of the road. The pickup shot by us and its driver laid on the horn, leaving us shaken and covered in his dust.

The remainder of the trip home was quiet, except for Mother's heavy breathing and her occasional attempt to impress upon me the fact that I had just nearly gotten us both killed.

In spite of my negative first attempt at driving Mother was willing to let me take the wheel the next time we ran an errand. Her dislike of driving seemed to outweigh her morbid fear that she might face death or dismemberment with me at the helm. I got better at wrestling the old Chevy, and eventually the rigors of a stick shift became second nature.

When I took driver's training a few years later, my instructor was quite resentful of my driving skill and suggested that I was perhaps a blatant little lawbreaker who had been on the road for years driving without a license. I hedged a bit and attributed my skill to years of driving the old hay truck and John Deere tractor. He pursed his lips and narrowed his eyes at me, and I was relegated to the back seat and a greener student took the wheel. For the remainder of the course I sat clutching the door handle and leaning into the side window as other students popped clutches and lurched toward ditches and slammed on brakes, pleasing the instructor with their desperate need of his guidance.

The years that followed brought more driving challenges, not so much from my driving ability, but from the derelict cars I drove.

One family car had a habit of losing all braking capacity at unexpected moments, and I learned to pump the pedal well in advance of a left turn in case I had to downshift and take evasive action.

Another car had a problem with changing gears upon demand, and I learned to leap out of the driver's seat at busy intersections, raise the hood, insert a screwdriver in the right gear and give it a flip, meshing it with another one and allowing me to go on my way as other cars honked a chorus behind me.

One temperamental Chevy tended to stall out at stop lights, and a faltering starter would only click when you turned the key, refusing to turn over and fire up the engine. I would grab a hammer, leap out, run around to the passenger side, throw myself onto the pavement and wiggle face-up under the car until I reached the front axle. Then I would locate the starter and give it a few loud whacks with my hammer, crawl out, leap back into the driver's seat and hold my breath as I turned the key. Usually that did the trick, and once again I would drive away amid a serenade of car horns behind me.

When Wayne and I married we drove a better class of car. His parents, Oldsmobile people with comfortable bank accounts, believed in trading in a car after a mere two years of driving it, replacing it with a shiny new one, an amazing concept to me. They would sell the old one to us at a charitably low price, and we would drive off with a beauty that had barely lost its new-car smell.

I wouldn't go back to the rusty Chevy days, preferring instead to drive vehicles with heaters that work, engines that start on cold winter days, and complicated equipment under the hood that I have never had the need to examine. But there is a part of me that misses the old wheezing hulks of my youth. They were a formidable challenge that taught me how to overcome adversity. They were not for the faint of heart, and they sent me into the world with a gleam in my eye and the conviction that I could handle life with a hammer and screwdriver and grease under my fingernails.

CHAPTER 5

NETTY HARRIMAN

Netty was larger than life. From her clothes to her giggle and red, drooping lips, she loomed above me like a helium cartoon character in a Rose Bowl parade. It wasn't the kind of looming that intimidated me or made me feel in any way inferior; it was more of a diversion in my otherwise lackluster life.

She lived with her parents and Boob and Dottie, so-called cousins who showed an unusual degree of affection for each other. Their house was a tiny square three-room shack covered in brown insul-brick. The roof sagged and the tiny front windows had handfuls of rags stuffed in the broken-out corners. It was dwarfed by an ancient pine tree that leaned over it protectively as if to compensate for its abysmal ugliness by shading it from the summer sun.

The whole family had an unsavory appearance. Pearl and Russell, Netty's parents, looked like they needed a bath, and when you got close enough to them, you could smell their pungent sweat and sour breath. They lived across the mile from our farm, and they drove Betty to school each day, unlike my parents who were of a mind that exercise was good and a mile walk in fresh air was not a particular disadvantage, a view I did not share.

Their old ford wheezed and rattled past our house each morning around seven-thirty, long before I was ready to leave for school, lunch sack in hand. As a result I hardly ever was able to hitch a ride with them and save myself a half-hour hike to the one-room school. On the days when I was ready early, I would dawdle at the end of the driveway and wait for the cloud of dust in the east to announce their appearance. Then I would walk purposefully down the road, feigning surprise when they stopped alongside me and invited me to ride with them.

Netty would open the rusty back door and scoot over next to Boob and Dottie and make room for me with a look of pure delight on her moon face. She seemed to think I moved in a social circle far above her own, and her adoring grin made me feel a little guilty for pretending to like her just to catch a ride to school.

There was hardly ever any conversation in the car as we rode along. The noise from the old car rattling over the chatter bumps in the sandy road drowned out any attempt to communicate, and I couldn't think of anything to say anyway.

Netty would sit beside me, and I could feel her grinning at me as she smoothed her gathered cotton skirt with plump, dimpled fingers. She wore bright red nail polish, something my mother frowned upon and felt was a bit worldly for proper Baptist girls under sixteen. I <u>was</u> allowed to wear clear polish with a slight hint of pink, but not the wildly seductive red I saw on Betty's nails. She chewed her nails, so there wasn't really that much area left to paint, but that didn't seem to diminish her pride in her colorful fingertips.

She wore lipstick, another worldly pleasure denied to me. It was applied in the general area of her full lips, covering them and spilling over a bit onto adjoining skin. Her teeth were usually streaked with a bit of bright color, giving her an intriguing look something like a woman in a Picasso painting I saw in an art book at school.

Upon our arrival at school, we would put our lunch sacks with the others on the narrow shelf above the coat hooks in the entryway. I took special note of where

Netty put her brown lunch bag - I wanted to make sure I didn't pick it up by mistake and unwrap the waxed paper that held her boloney and mustard sandwich on white Wonder Bread.

Then we would hurry outside and head toward the swings to fill the time until the other neighborhood kids arrived, something I felt would offer me more appealing social choices. In the meantime Netty would soar next to me in her swing, leaning back and grinning broadly as she sang out "Wheeeeeee" with unbridled joy.

As I remember Netty I feel a curious mixture of nostalgia and guilt. She was a pure soul who lived to please. The boundaries of her world were the few square miles that held her home and the school. I tried to be as kind as possible, feeling underneath my politeness that I was somehow smarter than her and would certainly go farther in the world. I hope I was kind enough.

CHAPTER 6

LITTLE OLD ALBERT

Little Old Albert was our closest neighbor to the west. He lived a mile away in a gray, weathered house that looked abandoned except for the occasional plume of smoke that rose from the chimney. The front yard was overtaken by goldenrod and fox tail grass and burdock. The driveway was little more than two parallel ruts through the weeds. Albert didn't own a car and he had too few visitors to keep the path open between the road and his back door.

He was small and stooped, barely five feet tall, and he shuffled slowly with one hand grasping his walking stick. He was nearly blind, and he suffered from a myriad of physical infirmities that kept him homebound and isolated.

Albert wore bibbed overalls and an old flannel shirt that was topped, summer and winter, by a denim jacket from Sears and Roebuck. Most of the buttons had long since fallen off, and he kept the front closed with three-inch nails lashed with binder twine. His high-top shoes had no laces, and he wound binder twine around the tops to keep them on.

He spoke in a voice barely above a whisper, and every second or third word was followed by "ah." He would come to our back door and say, "Hello Bernadine, ah, I, ah, wondered if, ah, Fred, ah, was home, ah." Mother would invite him into the kitchen to have a cup of coffee and a bite to eat, but he usually declined, too shy to try to hold a conversation, even with my kindly mother.

My parents looked out for Little Old Albert as best they could. Nearly every week Dad would stop on his way to Millington to do the grocery shopping and see if Albert needed anything from town. Sometimes Albert would be out of coffee or pet milk or canned beans or Quaker rolled oats, the staples of his diet. Dad would drop off the food on his way home, usually with a wedge of cheese wrapped in butcher's paper and a bag of cream-filled fudge drops.

Albert owned the biggest, blackest cats I had ever seen. They lived in the house with him, and he fed them raw

liver, his only extravagance. He worried that the social security people would find out that he used part of his meager disability check to feed cats, fearing they would stop
mailing him his monthly allowance and that he and his
cats would starve to death. Dad tried to reassure him that
he was not breaking the law, but Albert fretted anyway.

One day Dad was checking on Albert, and they
stood in Albert's kitchen next to the old wood range.
A granite coffee pot simmered on the stove, and Albert
was going over his usual concern about the use of gov-
ernment money to feed liver to cats when he glanced at
the big black coffee pot next to him. Between his preoccupation with his pets and his poor vision, he mistook
the pot for a cat and swatted it across the room saying,
"Scat, ah, you old cat, ah!"

There was something about Little Old Albert that
made most people act kindly toward him. The Juniata
Baptist Ladies' Aid Society frequently remembered him at
Christmas with things like food and new socks and gloves.
One year they made a patchwork quilt and voted to give it
to him to keep him warm on winter nights. They presented it to him and he murmured thanks and stared shyly at
his feet until they left. The next time Dad stopped by to
check on Albert, he noticed the quilt - but not on the bed
next to the kitchen table. Albert had carefully nailed it to
the floor and was proudly using it for a colorful rug.

During the summer Albert found occasion to walk to Juniata, three miles away, particularly when he was out of kerosene for his two-burner stove. He had to pass our house, and as he came into view by our line fence someone would spot his stooped figure shuffling along, a greasy vinegar jug clutched in front of him, a corn cob stuffed in the top. The first one to see him would yell "Here comes Little Old Albert," and we'd watch him inch his way toward our driveway. If Dad was home we would alert him that Albert was on his way to Warmbiers to buy a gallon of kerosene, and Dad would always find a reason to be driving there himself and would invite Albert to ride along. It was a delicate matter, and Dad was always careful to preserve Albert's pride; he stubbornly refused to accept what he called "charity."

Sometimes Albert would turn into our driveway, just to visit with "Fred, ah," or to return a dish of Mother's that had held one of her shared meals. I and my little sister Mary and baby sister Sally would hover near him, fascinated by his unique, dwarf-like body. His crusty clothes and the distinctive odor of kerosene mixed with wood smoke intrigued us. Mary, four years old, with her snappy chocolate eyes and tight black curls, was the brave one who would talk to him. Her voice carried better than ours, and he took notice of her and seemed to be at ease answering her questions about how he was doing. He invariably would fish a nickel out of his coat pocket and ask her if she, ah, would like to have it, ah, and she would gleefully take it and skip away to show it to Mother.

Sally, two years old, blond and blue eyed and apparently invisible to Albert, would shyly move closer, hoping he would find a nickel for her, but he never seemed to notice her. She would hover for a while, and I would nudge her a bit, encouraging her to make herself more visible, but she would lose interest, being too young to have developed an affection for money, and wander off to play with Lassie, our patient family dog.

For many years our quaint little neighbor shuffled in and out of our daily routine. Sometimes weeks would pass without sight of him, and Mother would send Dad down to make sure he was all right. When Dad returned with news that he was fine, we would breathe easier.

One night in late fall as I was getting ready to crawl into bed I looked out the west window toward Albert's house. With first curiosity then horror I saw an orange glow in the sky. It grew larger then erupted into yellow flames that leaped up into the darkness; Little Old Albert's house was on fire.

Within seconds Dad was in the car speeding toward Albert's rapidly burning home. We clustered at the upstairs window and watched with dreadful fascination as the flames shot into the sky and sparks like summer fireworks cascaded downward. The ancient old pine tree that leaned over the roof ignited, and the tree quickly became a silhouette of ribs and a tall, glowing trunk.

With surprising speed the house was consumed by the fire. The roof collapsed inward, sending plumes of sparks upward, then the fire ceased to rage and settled down to an orange glow. We watched with the horrible realization that Albert was in the midst of that fire, and we were certain that he was dead. In a brief span of time we had been jerked from our safe and sheltered world and plunged into a dark reality where death and destruction existed.

Finally we saw the lights of Dad's car as he approached our driveway. We ran to the back door, our hearts heavy with dread. Dad got out of the car, but instead of walking toward the house he moved to the passenger door and opened it. Slowly, with Dad's help, a stooped figure emerged; it was Little Old Albert! He clutched Dad's arm and leaned against him, dazed and bewildered. He was alive!

With unspeakable joy and relief we watched as Dad guided Albert toward the back door and helped him into the kitchen. He was incoherent and unable to grasp what had just happened. Mother and Dad gently led him into the living room and brought blankets and a pillow for the day bed where he could spend the remainder of the night. Mother sat in the rocking chair near his bed for the rest of the night in case he awoke and was terrified and didn't know where he was.

We learned the next day of Albert's escape from his burning home. The fire had started near the crumbling stone fireplace that stood in the center of the house. Perhaps rags or paper had ignited, but miraculously Albert had awakened before the fire spread. His night blindness prevented him from seeing anything except the glow of the fire, and he instinctively edged away from it. As he moved toward the door his hand fell on his mother's Bible that he kept on a small table. Clutching it, he backed out of the house, disoriented and bewildered. As the fire grew intense and the flames engulfed the structure, Albert shuffled backward, driven by the blistering heat.

The flames ignited the tall, dead grass around the foundation, and a ring of fire began to spread outward. As the flames approached Albert, he edged away, keeping a few feet between him and the burning grass.

It was there that Dad found him, a stooped figure in a ragged flannel night shirt, clutching a tattered book and edging backward from flames that licked toward him. Dad guided him toward the car and tried to explain what had happened, but Albert was too dazed to understand.

The next morning Albert gradually was able to comprehend the events of the previous night. He huddled in a chair and rocked gently back and forth, grief engulfing him as he realized that the only world he had ever known had disappeared in flames.

Mother wept with him and tried to comfort him and get him to eat, but he was inconsolable.

In the days that followed it became apparent that Albert needed a safe place to live and that we were unable to care for him. He needed constant attention and could not take care of himself. With great sorrow Dad arranged for him to be moved to the County Farm in Caro, a sprawling, gloomy old building that housed charity cases and disabled elderly people such as Albert.

Leaving Albert in the cold, sterile surroundings of the County Farm, confined to a metal cot in a ward of feeble, dying people broke my father's heart. There was no other way, but Dad's eyes showed the pain he felt for the action he had been forced to take.

He visited Albert as often as possible, taking him warm felt slippers and cookies and fudge drops, but Albert was listless and unresponsive, saying little more than "I want to sleep, ah, in my own bed, ah."

Albert lived a few short weeks in his final home, then he quietly died. We arranged for a grave in the Millington Cemetery, and Albert was laid to rest under a tall pine tree that whistled gently in the wind.

CHAPTER 7

GUINEAS

Guineas and I go back a long way. Their neat speckled bodies and tiny naked heads weave in and out of my childhood memories and conjure visions of dangerous encounters. Whenever guineas were present, I was in potential peril.

My parents, unlike me, had no qualms about living in close proximity to guineas. They embraced diversity in the chicken yard, and guineas held a special place in their hen hierarchy. Guineas were independent, wary, and they managed their lives with little or no assistance from humans. They perched in trees at night, foraged for their food by day, and acted as intruder alerts when visitors happened by. Their shrill staccato clamor demanded the attention of the homeowner and caused the visitor to cower and shrink back into his vehicle.

Guineas were a haughty species that disdained other fowls. They avoided social gatherings of mindless hens who scratched and pecked in summer yards and joyfully chased down insects and fought over their remains. Guineas were too dignified to engage in such behavior. They moved instead in a kind of stilted dance, sculpted bodies gliding smoothly as their blue-black heads bobbed up and down in search of food.

Even their eggs were distinctive, small, hard-shelled, shiny and brown, one end tapering to a point. My family rarely ate their eggs, since guineas spurned nesting boxes in the chicken coop and chose to lay their eggs in secret places we seldom happened upon. Unlike chickens that dropped their eggs in straw-filled cubicles with mindless regularity, guineas chose remote, sheltered spots in thickets of brush, lining their nests with soft bits of grass and their own feathers. They would fill the nest with twenty or more eggs, and then sit patiently for weeks, keeping the eggs warm and turning them with regularity.

The chicks were a source of amazement to me. These tiny, delicate creatures had developed inside the confines of a tough egg shell, pecked a hole in their prison wall, and enlarged it until they tumbled from their little spheres. Then standing up on fragile matchstick legs, they joined their parents in their eternal quest for food.

It was at this point that our worlds collided. Adult guineas were generally reclusive and aloof, avoiding confrontation rather than rushing into conflict – until they hatched their young. Then they became militant guardians of their chicks, their heads bobbing up and down as their beady little eyes searched for threats to their offspring. Anyone who moved within twenty feet was subject to swift and merciless attack, made more terrifying by the piercing racket they created.

As a small child I learned to give them wide berth when they were raising a family. But sometimes I would be distracted, or I'd come around the corner of the tool shed without a cautious first peek, and I would step right into their private domain. In a flurry of steel gray feathers they would swoop down on me, flogging and pecking my bare legs as I fled shrieking and cringing. When they were satisfied that I had retreated far enough to suit them they would fluff their feathers and settle them back down into little sleek mounds and set about to gather up their young who had hidden themselves while their parents waged war.

Another potential minefield I had to navigate was the chicken yard immediately outside the coop door. The guineas sensed that I was the designated egg gatherer and the closest Rogers' child to their own size. This seemed to give them valor that they didn't exhibit around the larger folks on the farm. They would deliberately lie in wait each late afternoon when I entered the coop to gather the day's eggs. They would saunter nonchalantly in the outer yard, pecking at bugs and eyeing me over their shoulders. When I came out of the door with a bucket of eggs I would find them ringing my escape path, poised and eager for battle. If I fled back into the coop they would only stroll nearby and bide their time. I had no choice but to pick up my heels and run like my life depended on it, which seemed to be a realistic assessment of the situation.

I would hear a barrage of raucous noise and feel their wings and beaks and sharp toenails on the backs of my legs as I fled for safety.

This ritual torture continued until the chicks were nearly full-grown. Then I could begin to relax and breathe easier in the hen yard. Gradually the adults lost their zeal for warfare and made fewer and fewer assaults on my young legs whenever I happened into their domain.

Life settled back into relative calm and I became the small mistress of the chicken manor once more – at least until the next flock of guineas hatched.

CHAPTER 8

MRS. CRENSHAW

Most of the homes in the neighborhood of my childhood had been sitting on their crumbling foundations forever. There wasn't a lot of new building activity in the 1940's; you were born in the house your grandfather or great grandfather had built, and if your surroundings didn't please you, you put up a new coat of wallpaper and got on with life.

The exception to this pattern were the occasional new dwellings that sprang up in wooded, swampy areas that no one laid claim to and tried to farm. Sometimes these houses were small collections of salvaged lumber and sheets of corrugated roofing panels, and they stood sadly in the tag alders with sagging roofs and doors hung askew. They weren't built for longevity, but merely to give shelter until the occupants moved on in search of a better dream.

When the Crenshaws, however, decided to build on the edge of the swamp north of our farm, they had hopes of putting down permanent roots. Mr. Crenshaw was a large, solid man who spoke very little and who worked like a plow horse – at least where building his house was concerned. He marked off the outline for the walls and dug trenches for shallow footings and stacked cement blocks for the task ahead. The walls edged upward, block by block, and he left large rectangles for the windows that he hoped to install later. The roof was added, flat and sloping downward toward the back door, and, finally, windows were puttied into place, smeared with remnants of insects and runoff from summer rainstorms.

Mother followed the progress with interest, looking forward to the day when the windows would be cleaned until they sparkled and crisp curtains were properly hung on straight, double rods. Unfortunately Mrs. Crenshaw didn't seem to share her passion for clean windows and curtains of any sort, properly hung or not. So Mother waited in vain and the curtainless windows collected spider webs and greasy film from the old cook stove. Eventually all you could see were mere outlines of the interior when you drove by and glanced at the windows facing the road.

Mrs. Crenshaw, either from a love of house plants or a desire for privacy, collected large, sprawling plants in galvanized buckets and placed them in the front windows. Following their natural yearning for sunlight, the plants leaned toward the dirty glass and struggled in all directions seeking the sun. The effect was a sort of jungle-like barrier between the curious eyes of passersby and the people who lived behind the walls.

After Mr. Crenshaw finished the house to his liking he stopped working, and we rarely saw him anywhere but sprawled in his lumpy recliner behind the leafy curtains, head back and mouth open in blissful sleep. It was left to Mrs. Crenshaw the task of tending to their four children and keeping the house from falling down around their ears.

She was unique in appearance - sturdy and short with a thick torso and a large head that sat farther ahead on her shoulders than you might expect. Her dark hair was wrapped tightly around her head and held in place with a heavy cotton hairnet. She twisted it into a knot in the middle of her forehead to keep loose hairs from escaping. The only other facial feature that caught your eye was a large mole centered an inch above her eyebrows, giving her face a curious symmetry.

Her voice was husky and low, as if she were just getting over a chest cold. She was not gifted in the art of conversation, answering only when she was spoken to. Mother, a kind woman who gathered the unloved and abandoned to her bosom, took charge of Mrs. Crenshaw's social life and frequently invited her to ride along with us to Wednesday night prayer meeting or an occasional family function at the church. Since the Crenshaws did not own a car in running condition, Mrs. Crenshaw was happy to accept mother's offer. During those trips to and from church Mother did her best to hone her untalkative passenger's communication skills.

I sat in the back seat listening to the two women as they tried to exchange pleasantries. Mostly Mother offered pleasant topics for consideration, and Mrs. Crenshaw stopped them cold with a guttural snort or a brief, cynical observation. Sometimes her two younger children, Margie and Brucie, would ride along, and we'd sit in the backseat in uncomfortable silence, their conversational skills no better than their mother's.

Margie was a year older than me and Brucie a year younger. Both were gangly and thin, and their pale skin suggested a diet light on fruits and vegetables. Margie fidgeted a lot and scratched her head, prompting her mother to growl, "Quit pickin' at yer hair or Miz Rogers will think you have head lice." This would cause Brucie to snicker nervously, and his mother would snarl, "Shut up, Brucie!"

The only time Mrs. Crenshaw ever spoke directly to me occurred one Wednesday night when we were going to Vassar to pick up Dad after his afternoon shift was finished at the foundry. We were a one-car family, so if we needed the car ourselves Mother would have to drive Dad to work after the noon meal, then we would pick him up at eleven that evening.

The foundry ran two shifts, and after the last one the fire in the smelting area was put out until the next morning's shift began. A tall chimney over the furnace vented the heat and smoke, and when the fire was extinguished, flames and sparks would shoot up above the chimney, lighting the night sky.

That evening as we sat waiting for Dad to walk wearily toward the parking area carrying his empty black lunch box, I felt compelled to make small talk. "Do you know what my dad's job is in the foundry?" I asked.

"What?" she muttered.

"He stands up on that smokestack and shovels coal down into the fire to make the sparks shoot up that high," I said.

Then she replied with more enthusiasm than I had ever heard from her, "Liars have their place in the lake of fire."

I was certain I heard my mother snicker, but a hasty cough replaced it so quickly I couldn't be sure.

The ride home was quiet, except for an occasional "Ma, make Brucie quit grinnin' at me," followed by "I ain't grinnin', Ma," followed by "Shut up, Brucie."

The only time in my memory that Mrs. Crenshaw directed her "Shut up" order at Margie occurred during one trip to the church for a revival meeting. Mother was, as usual, talking about household matters like gardening and cooking. She mentioned potatoes, and how our family enjoyed then in any form or recipe. Mrs. Crenshaw snorted, "My kids don't eat potatoes."

Margie chirped from the backseat, "We'd eat 'em, Ma, if you'd cook 'em."

Mrs. Crenshaw put that notion to rest with a sharp "Shut up, Margie."

The other Crenshaw children were boys, Wesley and Eldon, much older and in their twenties. Eldon, the eldest, attended a Bible School and found a young woman who agreed to marry him. She seemed pleasant, and the two of them showed remarkable promise. The wedding was held at the church in Juniata, and the reception was hosted at the Crenshaw home in the swamp. We were eager to get our first look at the inside of the house, and to see what Mrs. Crenshaw considered a proper reception for her son and his new bride.

We parked at the side of the narrow dirt road, along with several other dutiful neighbors, and made our way toward the front door. It was evident from the dirty front windows that house cleaning wasn't considered a necessity for a proper reception. A few naked light bulbs lit up the interior, revealing a sagging horse-hair sofa, Mr. Crenshaw's lumpy recliner, and a few mismatched kitchen chairs arranged around the room for guests. The kitchen table held a stack of paper plates, forks, and several pies that were apparently substitutes for a wedding cake.

Mother chatted with the bride and groom and the groups of neighbors that stood in uncomfortable clusters, and when it became apparent that no one was in charge of the customary rituals of a wedding reception, Mother stepped in.

"Shall I cut the pie and serve the guests?" she asked Mrs. Crenshaw.

"I suppose so," came a brusque reply.

Mother found a butcher knife and began to cut the pie and lift pieces onto the paper plates nearby. "Help yourselves," she announced cheerfully. We lined up and took a plate and fork. I wondered what kind of pie I was looking at, never having seen one in the past that was quite this color and texture. The filling was grainy and the color of the rust that collected in the bottom of the horse trough. The crust was gray and crumbly. "Dig in!" Mother said optimistically, and I knew that meant "Take a bite and act like you like it or you will answer to me when we get home."

After the first bite everything got a little uncertain. I realized soon after the initial forkful that I was eating something from the squash or pumpkin family that had been mashed and spread, sugarless, onto an uncooked pie crust. I tried not to make eye contact with the others in the room who were experiencing the same peculiar sensation as they sampled the wedding pie. I eventually had no choice but to swallow, as did the others around me, and a flurry of activity erupted in which everyone explained the reasons why they had to leave early, and how sorry they were that they could not stay longer, and could they please take their pie with them to finish when they got home.

Mother dallied a bit, tidying up and admiring the modest gifts that Eldon and his bride were opening and displaying on the couch. Mrs. Crenshaw came as close to pleasure as I had ever seen as she watched from the shadows. Apparently the reception met all her expectations, and she wasn't offended by the early departure of the guests.

The unorthodox reception turned out to be the highlight of the Crenshaw's social calendar. Wesley moved away and we heard little about him, his mother seemingly knowing no more than we did when we inquired. Margie and Brucie grinned their way through elementary school, and if they went to high school they rode a different bus than I did, and I never saw them again.

Their old cement block house has settled a bit in the swamp, and the roof has caved in over the back porch. The windows still stare darkly at the road, and, having reached the maximum coating of dirt, they look about the same as they did in 1949 when Mother cut Eldon's wedding pie.

CHAPTER 9

THE HAIRY ARM

I was introduced to the hairy arm in the tender days of my youth. I lived with my family on a farm in the dark part of Tuscola County. The days were of normal brightness, but the nights were inky and shrouded in black velvet. When the sun went down the light was sucked out of our world and the air was filled with deepest ebony, like a suffocating pile of crow feathers. It was here in this absence of light that the hairy arm lived.

We valiantly fought back with sickly incandescent light bulbs. At night the house filled up with pale yellow light that leaked out of the windows for a few feet. A black switch by the back door turned on a single bulb hanging under a green shade in the peak of the tool shed halfway between our house and the cow barn. It produced a perfect circle of comfort on the yellow sand of the driveway beneath. But everywhere else it was deepest night.

I was not a night child. My brother and older sisters disappeared through the black curtain and their happy cries of pursuit and discovery reached me in the living room, but I had no desire to join them. I felt a grim premonition of doom and I was always surprised when they came through the back door smiling and smelling of sweaty fun.

My journeys into the night were never voluntary. The rare nocturnal trip to the outhouse under the scrub apple tree occurred when I misjudged nature's calling and forgot to tend to business before the last traces of light faded away. Then I would wheedle an older sister into standing guard nearby while I disappeared into the weathered outhouse for as short a time as possible. I'd shoot out of the door and sprint back to the house, surprised to have escaped doom lurking in the dark.

The only other reason for going outdoors after dark was to attend to duties in the barn. From late fall to early spring it was impossible to get the cows fed and tended to while it was still light. Usually my older brother took care of that job, but sometimes I was forced into service when he was busy with something else. "Polly, run out and feed the cows," Mother would say casually. My heart would pound and my palms would get sweaty.

"Can't Norma do it?" I'd ask futilely, knowing full well I only got elected when there was no other possibility.

"Oh, you'll be fine; just don't think about it," she would say with oily confidence. "I'll stand here by the window and watch while you are outside."

My mother was a truthful woman, but she was easily distracted. I knew she'd stand there for a few moments, then remember something that absolutely required her immediate attention, and there'd she go. I'd return later and listen to her lamely explain how she had stepped away only a few seconds earlier.

It was on one of these nights when I did the barn chores that I met the hairy arm. The trip started out in the usual way. I turned on the tool shed light as I went through the back door, the old screen door creaking shut behind me. Then down the big cement steps, past the wood shed where the cats slept, and into the comforting circle of light in front of the tool shed. Beyond that was the black vacuum of the barn yard and the iron latch on the big wooden door of the barn. Just inside the barn, above and to the right, in a recessed window frame clogged with dusty cobwebs, was the switch that turned on the barn lights. Once I had turned on the lights I could breathe easier for a short time.

The cows were large and warm and docile, and I liked poking hay into the mangers and listening to them methodically chomp their supper. The aromatic smell of dried alfalfa mixed with the earthy and strangely pleasant smell of fresh cow manure always filled me with mild delight. I'd stand and breathe in the smells until I remembered that I had to return to the house through the zone of doom.

Then reluctantly, like a child walking toward her mother who had just demanded coldly, "Polly, come here this minute!" I'd return to the barn door. With one hand holding the iron latch, I'd reach upward with the other and turn the lights off. A quick slam of the door and a dropping of the latch into place left me outside where I was swallowed up in darkness.

Now began the inner turmoil. My logic told me there was nothing around me that wasn't there in daylight. No toothy creatures lurked behind the bushes, salivating as they watched me through pale green eyes. No eight-foot escaped convicts were edging toward me, bent on grabbing me and stuffing me into the burlap bags slung over their shoulders. No large birds sat hunched in the trees, planning to swoop down and grab me in their enormous curved beaks, sweep me off the ground and carry me back to their nests to feed their young.

I knew all this in my head. But in my heart I knew I was in grave danger from something that was waiting out there, something sinister and hungry, and that there was a chance it would get me before I could reach the back door.

I began the death march toward the house. One leaden foot in front of the other, I moved toward the circle of light in front of the tool shed. Once there, I felt dubious relief. I was safe for the moment, but whatever waited for me in the dark had the leisure of circling and sizing me up for the kill. I could not stay there until morning; I might as well get eaten sooner than later.

The moment I stepped out of the circle of light I knew whatever was out there was no longer just toying with me. "Don't run," I told myself. Somehow I knew that if I bolted and ran I was fair game and it would nab me and that would be that. But panic quickly overtook reason, and I fled toward the house, heart pounding and legs rubbery. Now I felt hot breath on my heels. It was loping along, enjoying the chase and savoring the moment when it was going to pounce.

The house seemed miles away, but miraculously I climbed up the back steps and shot through the screen door. Just as I crossed the line from blackness into light I felt a breeze as something swiped at my ankles, missing them by a hair. Gasping my way into the kitchen, I was met by Mother who smiled guiltily and murmured something about checking a pot on the stove.

Sitting in the living room later with Volume Two of Child Craft on my lap, I tried to sort out what had just happened. Before tonight I had only a vague sense of doom, a general feeling that something lurked in the night that I didn't ever want to meet up with. But this time I had met it on a far more personal level than I wanted to. Hot breath on my ankles was more than a vague fear - it came from something hungry with big teeth and eyes that never blinked.

I tried to divert my mind with poems that swept me into new worlds, like The Highwayman with "pistol butts all a-twinkle...and a bunch of lace at his chin." Even Pirate Don Durk of Dowdee failed to capture my attention, and tonight he seemed pale and uninteresting. The Raggedy Man who works fer Pa, however, caught my eye; he told Lizabuth Ann about "the Squidgicum-Squees 'at swallers therselves," and "the hole 'at the Wunks is got, 'at lives way deep in the ground." So I wasn't the only one who had trouble with scary creatures!

What <u>was</u> this menace in the night, I wondered as I crawled into bed later. Sleep came slowly and brought with it dreams of things that rustled and lurked in hot, breathless caves or around dark corners. I awoke the next morning with fuzzy cobwebs of memory fading in the bright sunlight.

I ran outside and looked at a world that was safe and cheerful. John Deere tractors stood where black mounds of terror had huddled the night before. Lilac bushes and day lilies lined the driveway instead of monsters whose stomachs growled with hunger. Around the corner of the back porch were only grass and sunshine and a puddle of water from the back room drain.

I was joyous. I ruled my world again. I took up my crooked poking stick and headed to the creek to agitate crayfish out of the shadows of rocks in the shallow water. The day stretched endlessly ahead of me and I was safe.

Then without warning it was night again.

Mother's voice was a cold knife in my heart. "Polly, run out and feed the cows." Like a prisoner on her way to the gallows I trudged through the darkness to the barn. Maybe I was too distracted by the misery that bubbled up in my chest to notice, but suddenly

I realized that nothing was dogging my steps. I went through the weathered gray door and pitched alfalfa into the mangers.

My trip back to the house was not so tranquil. That old prickly feeling on the back of my neck returned as I left the barn. Don't run, I told myself. It will get you if you run. Self-control petered out about twenty feet from the back door and I bolted and ran. There it was again, inches from my heels, fetid breath on my ankles. I shot through the screen door, limp with terror.

This deadly chase through the dark became a familiar pattern. With grim resignation I faced peril each time I had to venture out into darkness. Every time I successfully eluded my pursuer I patted myself on the back and hoped that that was the end of my ordeal. But why, I wondered, was I threatened only when I returned to the safety of the back door? Then I figured it out; this menace was more interested in the chase than the capture. He enjoyed my misery more than he wanted to bag me.

So how did I outsmart this wretch? It came to me after one particularly brisk sprint for the screen door. I had bolted and run like a scalded cat, and he nearly got me. Like a light bulb turning on in my brain I saw my way out; don't run. Simple as that. Saunter and drive him crazy. Take away all his fun. Dawdle and give him nothing to chase.

It wasn't easy, but I did my best. When I reined in my urge to sprint he slouched and pouted in the shadows. When I gave in to panic and ran he was right there behind me, hot breath on my ankles and glee in his heart. So I practiced whistling and sauntering, and to my amazement I learned that there was a chance I might win the war.

About this time I got a better fix on what I was up against. At first he had seemed to be of giant proportions, three times bigger than me and teeth the size of boulders. But then I began to figure out what he was. He was an arm. A stocky, muscled arm with a huge hand on the end. It was covered sparsely in coarse, black hair, even on his fingers, and it had long, yellowed nails that curved under in bony arcs. He had no head, no legs, just an arm that could somehow move quicker than I could.

Once I had figured this out, I somehow managed to deal with it better. Not that the hairy arm let up and left me alone. He still hunkered down in the dark and waited for me to venture out and give him the pleasure of a good chase. But I wore down and couldn't maintain the same level of terror every time I met up with him.

I even started to forget about him on rare occasions. Once every so often I would walk through the back door at a normal pace and realize that I hadn't even noticed him skulking behind me.

As I got braver he seemed to get less terrifying. I sensed disappointment and a growing sadness in him as our races slowed down and got less intense. Then he stopped waiting for me around the corner of the porch. Suddenly there was nothing there but the dark. No creature eyeing me and waiting to pounce. Just empty shadows. I was limp with relief.

I should have known he wouldn't give up that easily. I had him beaten him in the dark outside the back door, but he sized up the situation and came at me from another angle. He moved into the basement.

Now our basement was a place you only visited when you had to. The floor was dirt and the walls were stone and crumbling mortar. When you went down the steps you had to duck at the bottom or you would hit your head on a huge support beam above you. Then you walked down a wide, sloping plank and you were in the main room of the basement. The center of the room was filled with a tall, steel-flanked furnace that heated the house above. There we poked wood through the heavy iron door and into the firebox to keep us warm in the winter.

The back half of the room was filled with stacks of wood that Dad had split and stacked during warm weather. Two walls were lined with sagging wooden shelves held up by cement blocks where Mother kept the canned food. There she arranged Mason jars filled with peaches and pears and applesauce and dill pickles and strawberry jam and green beans and beef.

The rafters were low and anyone over five feet tall had to hunch over or he'd whack his head when he walked. A single naked light bulb hung in front of the furnace, and you had to reach up and screw it in to turn on the light.

It was damp and musty and you went down and came up as quickly as possible and shut the old wainscoted door behind you with relief.

The steps were wide planks, open at the back and smooth from years of use. Behind the steps was a crawl space under the kitchen with piles of rock and yellow clay. In the far corner was an old water pump that occasionally sprang to life and filled a holding tank that stood nearby. The lead pipes that connected the tank to the kitchen sink would rattle and clatter when anyone turned on the cold water faucet above. If you happened to be going up or down the steps at that moment it would give you quite a start.

One evening when I had settled in for a few chapters of The Hardy Boys' latest adventure, Mother called from the kitchen, "Polly, run down in the cellar and bring up a quart of pickles."

I wondered, as usual, why she always told me to "run" somewhere. Run to cellar. Run to the barn. Run out to the garden. I never ran but merely shuffled, but she didn't seem to notice.

So down to the cellar I went. My descent into darkness made the hair stand up on the back of my neck. This felt different than the outdoor menaces that lurked in the shadows of the yard. It seemed closer and more dangerous, like something with long spider legs that might drop down the back of my shirt, or a snake coiled and ready to strike from its hiding place in the wood pile.

I picked up the nearest quart of pickles, unscrewed the light bulb, and made my way back to the rectangle of yellow light at the top of the stairs. Suddenly that old urge to bolt and run overcame me, and I pounded up the steps and shot into the kitchen. Mother looked my way with curiosity but said nothing. She was always gracious toward me in my moments of cowardice and mad flight, mostly because, I had observed, she was even more cowardly than I was and needed to stay in my good graces lest she might have to take trips into the dark herself.

I settled back down with the Hardy Boys and it suddenly hit me what had just happened. The hairy arm, which I thought had given up and slunk back to his lair, had moved into the basement and was lurking under the steps. A heavy sense of doom overcame me as I faced a future of peril and pursuit.

Days later I was once more sent to the basement for something Mother deemed necessary. Down the steps I went, waiting for the onslaught, but nothing happened. On the trip back up the stairs, however, I felt the overpowering presence of something between the top step and the kitchen floor. My legs were too short to take two steps at a time, and as I approached the top one I felt the old whiff of wind as the hairy arm timed his swipe at my ankle. Missing me by a hair, he retreated back into the dirt piles to bide his time until my next visit to the cellar.

So it was certain; the hairy arm had moved indoors. Now he lived under the same roof as me. He could lounge down there in the darkness and just wait for me. Every time I had to go to the cellar he could dawdle behind the stairs until I had to return to the kitchen, and then he could grab at my ankles for pure pleasure.

It seemed far more unsettling to realize that only the downstairs floor separated him from me. If he could live in my basement, where else might he decide to move? Would I have to deal with him under the kitchen table? In my dresser drawers? Behind the couch? When he lived outdoors I thought there was a greater chance I might elude him; there were more places for him to lie in wait, and he couldn't possibly cover every one of my possible paths to the back door. But now his target had narrowed to a few feet of air space behind the top step of the basement stairs. A heavy sense of doom descended upon my heart.

In spite of the new peril under the basement stairs I learned to get on with life. My older sisters were amused by my misery, and on those occasions when I would lose all self-control and pound madly up the steps and into the kitchen gasping for breath, they would say with casual disdain, "Hairy arm nearly got you, huh?"

But for the most part I learned how to grit my teeth and control my mad impulse to dash for safety. It was of particular importance for me to avoid bolting into the kitchen in the wintertime, since the old cast iron cook stove was just a few feet from the kitchen door and in a direct line with an object hurtling out of the cellar. A preoccupation with saving my ankles from the hairy arm made me more prone to forget to turn sharply to the right, and I had more than one superficial burn to nurse in those days.

Then, just when I thought things couldn't get any worse, they did. One hot summer night as I lay sweltering on damp sheets trying to get to sleep, I hung my arm over the mattress and swung it a bit to generate a breeze. The old fear gripped my heart, and just as I yanked my arm back from the void, I felt the familiar breeze as the hairy arm swiped at me from under the bed. He had moved upstairs!

This was not what my young heart needed to know. The enemy had become mobile. He lived under my bed, skulking there while I slept above, waiting for me to flop a limb over the edge of the mattress so he might leisurely swipe away at it.

The nights that followed were harrowing indeed. I concentrated on lying in the center of the mattress, as far as possible from the fateful edge.

The summer nights left us limp and listless in our steamy old farm house. My room had one small window that faced the north, and any summer breeze rarely came from that direction. One tiny window fan was installed in my parents' room, and any moving air it created fizzled out long before it reached my room. So

I flopped and sweltered and longed for sleep through summer heat waves, and now I had this new misery to deal with.

For a while I felt doomed. Held captive on my mattress, I dreaded waking in the middle of the night to find that I had accidentally dangled a limb over the edge of the bed like bait for the creature that lurked beneath. But then I determined somehow that my foe followed rules. He would never menace me while I was sleeping. And the sheet was a magic barrier that he never crossed. So if I wrapped my arm or leg in the top sheet I could safely dangle it over the edge of the bed and not fear the swipe from the darkness underneath.

The nights that followed turned slowly into years. I grew skillful at facing days with casual bravery, safe from the threat of my old arch enemy, then shifting to nights laced with a lurking menace that dogged my steps and swiped at my heels when he pleased.

How I survived childhood with a hairy arm in hot pursuit is a wonder to me. But with each passing year I got better at facing fear. Eventually I grew up and left my childhood home, moving into a college dorm where the nights were pushed back by the glow of mercury vapor lights. The hairy arm had no place to hide and I breathed easier. But I missed him in a strange way. He was a formidable foe that toughened me up and taught me how to face danger.

When I married and Wayne and I moved into our farm house in the country, I was displeased to find the old basement was not much of an improvement over my parents' dank cellar. The steps were open in the back, and behind them stood the old holding tank that rattled and made me leap when the outside well began pumping water. The single light bulb at the bottom of the stairs required a yank on the chain to turn it on. Going down the stairs was bearable, but on the trip back to the kitchen I had to pull the chain and ascend the steps in blackness.

On one trip up from the basement I felt the old childhood panic that made me bolt and run into the kitchen wide eyed and gasping for breath. This cannot be, I told myself. I am a grown woman with children; I am too old to be chased by childhood monsters. But there he was, the hairy arm, leering and skulking under my basement steps.

For months he delighted in harassing me and testing my mettle. Sometimes I won, sometimes he did. This had to change. One day I contrived to hire an electrician to do some maintenance work and while he was there I had him install a switch at the top of the stairs, and with glee I removed the pull chain from the light bulb below.

I assumed that was the end of the hairy arm. Not so. Years later we remodeled the upstairs and had a small door installed to connect the back of a closet to the storage under the eaves. It lacked a door knob, having, instead, a small latch and "O"closure. On one trip into the attic I returned to the closet, hunched over and pulling the door shut behind me. Before I could latch it I realized with childish horror that the old enemy was lurking in the dark and was ready to pounce. Losing my poise, I yanked the door shut with such force that it swung backward into the black attic. Now I had a choice. I could give in to terror and run, leaving the door gaping open, or I could act my 50 years and calmly reach in, retrieve the latch, and close it with dignity. I chose the latter.

It was with a certain degree of sadness that I sensed the hairy arm slink away to hide beneath the eaves, vanquished by the prey he had so faithfully stalked all those years.

I never encountered the hairy arm again. Even when I am walking to the garage on a starless night and I leave the comfort of the back door light and enter the shadows I do not sense his presence. It wasn't my intention to totally defeat him. I only wanted to live in peace with him. Whatever his faults, he fought fair. I always knew where I stood and what I was up against. Like a cantankerous old hound dog chasing a cat, he was more interested in pursuing me than catching me. In a strange sort of way I think I enjoyed the game as much as he did. I developed a grudging admiration for my old enemy. He gave me many memorable moments of heart-stopping thrills, and I hope that somewhere he is poised at the edge of darkness waiting to take a swipe at some unsuspecting kid who had to run out and feed the cows.

CHAPTER 10

THE LADIES' AID SOCIETY

Mama bellowed at me from the back porch like an old bull. "Ruth Ann Rogers, get in the house this minute!" I could tell she was serious from her tone. Sometimes she called to me and her voice was softer, more like thunder too far away to be scary. But when I was in real trouble her voice was very loud and cold and sharp, and I knew I'd better skedaddle up the creek bank and get to the back door on a dead run.

She grabbed one of my pigtails and gave it just enough of a pull to make me squinch my eyes shut and suck in my breath.

"Yes, Mama," I said, trying to sound brave and innocent. I knew why she was ready to scalp me. It was

82

Thursday afternoon, and only two hours before the Ladies' Aid Society were due to arrive for their monthly meeting, and the dishes were still sitting on the kitchen table with spaghetti sauce drying into red clumps and milk getting stinky in the glasses.

"Do the dishes and make the kitchen sparkle," she had said as we finished lunch that noon.

"Yes, Mama," I had replied without enthusiasm. "Doing the dishes" meant filling the tea kettle from the hand pump in the back room, lighting a match and holding it on the back burner of the kitchen stove and hoping the blue flame didn't pouf and singe my eyebrows. Then it was wait until steam came out of the spout, pour the hot water into the dish pan, and wash dishes for eight people which took forever.

I hated washing dishes. It made my fingers white and wrinkled, and the water never stayed warm, and when I got to the pans the soap bubbles would be gone and clumps of grease would be floating on the gray water. But I had to do it. When Mama gave an order in a certain tone, I hopped to it.

It seemed like a whole day later, but the dishes were washed and put away, the floor was swept, and all the clutter on the table was taken care of.

Just in time! A car rolled up the driveway, with two others right behind. Julia, Ruthie, Olive, and Betty got out of the first one. Julia beat them to the back door. She liked to be first so she could look around our house without any distraction and give it one of her fussy inspections. Her own house looked like a pig pen, but she expected everyone else's to be squeaky clean.

The others followed her into the back room and pretty soon everyone was talking and laughing and telling Mama how nice her house looked and how much they loved her curtains.

Mama's curtains were her claim to fame. They crisscrossed each window with deep ruffles and were freshly ironed even if she had to stay up all night to finish them. The ruffles on the double rod had to be just so. Mama would slide them back and forth until they suited her, cocking her head sideways until she was sure they were perfect.

Mama told us, "Judge not lest ye be judged," and she tried to live up to her own advice. But women who were slouchy and hung sloppy curtains got no respect from Mama. "You can tell what's in a woman's heart by the way she hangs her curtains," she'd say when we were driving into town. I'd be looking at the swing sets in the back yards and paved sidewalks with kids on shiny bikes, but Mama would be checking out everyone's curtains and deciding who hung them to suit her.

Mama's curtains and everything else passed inspection by the ladies and soon everyone was seated in the living room waiting for Josephine to call for order and open with prayer. I peeked around as she prayed, and with everyone else's eyes closed, I could check things out without getting a dirty look from someone.

Julia had a run up the side of one of her nylons, and I nearly snickered when I saw it. She was so uppity about other people's little flaws you'd have thought she had none of her own. I knew better, because I saw her house many times when I was staying overnight with Wanda, her granddaughter, and we'd go across the road and visit Julia.

Her kitchen smelled like old bacon grease, and her bathroom was positively grubby. We just had an old outhouse under the apple tree in the back yard, so I <u>was</u> impressed with the flush toilet in the storage room off the kitchen. But beyond that I didn't really admire her so-called bathroom. Besides, she stored eggs in large cardboard boxes just inside the door, and you could smell chicken poop and musty straw when you went in.

She hung her husband Fred's clothes on big nails pounded into the walls next to the commode, and his underwear was yellow and dingy. Mama would have had a fit if Dad's underwear looked like that. She'd have soaked things in Roman Cleanser water until they sparkled, or else cut them up and used them for mop rags.

After Josephine had said amen the ladies all shifted in their chairs and resituated themselves for the business meeting.

Mama asked if anyone had anything for the group to discuss, and they spent a long time deciding if they should send more support to Brother Brauers in Africa because it was so close to his furlough time and he'd be able to raise his own money speaking at local churches and taking up free-will offerings when he was back in Michigan.

Finally Mama reminded the ladies that the monthly support for Kim Chu was due. Kim Chu was an orphan in Korea, and every month Mama sent a check for ten dollars to World Vision to pay her expenses at the orphanage. Mama sometimes had a hard time collecting enough money by the due date, but she always found enough money of her own to make up the difference. She loved Kim Chu, and she never once missed a payment.

Mama didn't have much money of her own because Dad handled all the finances and even did the grocery shopping at Cobbs' Store in Millington every Saturday morning. He would buy anything she wrote down on the list, so we would have treats like Vernor's floats after the housecleaning was finished on Saturday afternoon and canned figs for Sunday morning breakfast. But she never had any money of her own for things like payments to World Vision. To provide money for such needs, she would sell extra eggs to a neighbor, and she'd keep the change that fell out of Dad's overalls and showed up in the bottom of the Maytag wringer washer on laundry day. Somehow Mama managed to find enough money to pay support for her Korean "daughter."

Pretty soon Josephine suggested that the ladies meet their responsibilities and honor the Lord by giving Mama their share of the monthly support, and the meeting came to a close.

Now came my favorite part, refreshments. Mama thanked the Lord for the blessings of food, and we eagerly headed for the dining room. Everyone loved to eat at Mama's table. She fixed things that were pretty and colorful and tasted so good you could hardly wait to get the next bite in your mouth. Even Julia told Mama how beautiful her table looked with the lace tablecloth covered by such beauty that it was a shame to help her-self and mess up the banquet which was as pretty as a picture.

Mama smiled and said it was really nothing special, just a few things from the garden and the orchard and her baking cupboard, but I knew she was pleased.

Julia filled her plate so high she had to squish some things together so they wouldn't fall off in her lap when she sat down. Later when everyone was full and there would be enough leftovers to feed everyone again, Julia would ask if she might take a bite or two home to poor Fred who wasn't feeling well and would be cheered up by Mama's good cooking. Mama would say of course and would give Julia a paper plate, and Julia would heap enough on it to feed both of them for a week.

It was a joke we giggled about when Julia wasn't around, how "poor Fred" was never feeling well and how a plate of food that Julia didn't have to pay for or cook would cheer him right up. Fred was a big, strong man who hardly ever seemed to be feeling poorly, but Julia worried about him all the time.

The last time the Ladies' Aid met, it had been Julia's turn to have everyone at her house. She cooked chick-en because the laying hens were ready to molt and had pretty much stopped laying, so eating one or two of them seemed to be more economical than feeding them until they decided to lay eggs again. She cut the chickens up in small pieces and made sure she had just enough to go around. She didn't believe in extravagance, and she always tried to match the number of servings with the number of ladies at her table.

Just about the time the ladies were ready to begin eating, the front door opened and Veva shuffled through. Julia looked stricken and her face turned pink, but she tried to be polite in front of her friends.

Veva was a distant relative of Julia's, and she and her husband Dell lived in a ramshackle house just down the road from Julia. Veva was only about four and a half feet tall, and she had one short leg that caused her to walk with a shuffle and a lurch. She was plump and wore a dirty, shapeless dress that came nearly to the top of her old work boots that had no laces.

Veva's house was a wreck. The roof had settled down over the back lean-to, and most of the windows were broken out and covered with cardboard nailed to the frames. The dirt floor was heaped with old clothes and empty tin cans and smelly trash. A couple of skinny dogs slunk around and hid behind the wood stove when anyone stopped by.

No one ever called except for Dad and the Mennonites. Dad sometimes dropped off food from the garden or brought a meal that Mama had fixed and had enough to share. The Mennonites came once every spring and bravely shoveled out the garbage, scrubbed the table and few pieces of furniture, and changed the bedding. They would replace last year's bedding with clean sheets and a new quilt that the ladies had pieced together. Then they would take the old bedding out behind the house and burn it along with the rest of the garbage.

Veva never felt the need to bathe or wash her clothes, and when she came into a room everyone knew it right away. So when Veva showed up in Julia's doorway we all held our breath and stopped talking. Julia told Veva that the Ladies' Aid was meeting, but Veva just stood there looking in at the refreshment table and fidgeting. Finally Julia asked her in a strange voice that sounded like she was choking if she'd like to come in and have a bite.

Veva shuffled past Julia and grabbed a plate. She started at the platter of chicken and took three of the biggest pieces. She took two pieces of chocolate cake, then she piled a big heap of strawberry Jello in the bare spot in the middle. As she started to walk away, the chicken caught her eye again, and she forked up another piece.

Poor Julia was frantic by now, because there weren't going to be enough pieces left to go around even once. She asked Veva if she wouldn't rather have some pork and beans or a piece of corn bread, but Veva answered happily, "Chicken's good enough for me."

That pretty much finished the refreshment time. Some of the women said that they had just had a big lunch before they came, and they'd only nibble on a dill pickle or two, and the rest were not too happy about eating chicken after Veva had touched it with her dirty fingers. So Julia had lots of leftovers to feed "poor Fred" who wasn't feeling at all well that day.

When we left to go home I waited for Mama to say something about poor Julia's ordeal, but she just murmured something to herself about Christian charity and not taking pride in ourselves as if we were better than others, and how our own righteousness was as filthy rags in the eyes of the Lord.

CHAPTER 11

PIGEON RIVER MAGIC

The road to the river meandered through the Pigeon River State Forest in northern Lower Michigan. It was flanked with timbered-off hills choked with young birch and poplar. Further on we passed through stands of white pine, oak, and maple beneath which dark ferns made a lacy, knee-deep carpet. Blackberry thickets bristled beside the trail, their hard green berries waiting for the suns of August to ripen them. The country rolled gently in waves of green, cut by the sandy ruts of the trail.

We came suddenly into a meadow filled with white daisies spread before the sun like bright sheets. Beyond the meadow a line of dark green tag alders bordered the clear water of the Pigeon.

Shutting off the engine of the van, we savored the sounds and smells of the meadow before unloading our gear. The strident call of a Jay was mellowed by the softer chirping of song birds. The singing of invisible insects pulsated in the warm mid-morning air. Updrafts of sun-warmed air carried the smell of strawberry and moss and spicy fern.

We grew eager to fish. We spread out our gear and dressed quickly in our waders and vests, filling our pockets with little metal cases whose compartments held devices of rich and mysterious meaning. Taking up our rods and reels, we moved to the river.

It lay between the double rows of willow and tag alder like a rich amber jewel. Moving down the bank and stepping into the clear water was like coming home after a long and solemn absence. The cold water pushed against us and rubber waders clung to our legs like gloves.

To wade once more into a deep, strong river brings a quiet peace that seldom comes to those who move about in cities of concrete, glass, and steel. To lean into the current, to feel the tug and pull of its eddies, to plant one's feet firmly among smooth rocks and to stand quietly as the current washes one clean – that is to feel the unexpected joy of one who has been allowed to return home after a long exile.

Wayne preferred to fish upstream, so I moved away from him, letting the current nudge me downstream. Around a bend the river flattened out before me, its deep, swirling waters changing to sparkling riffles. A heron, fishing the shallows, exploded upward in a frenzy of indignation as I came into sight.

The rent in the silent cloak of the morning was quickly mended, and I moved on to the next bend which led me once again into deeper waters.

I cast a fly tentatively, letting it float lazily toward the place where the water swirled and darkened over a log. Suddenly I realized with annoyance that I had left my landing net behind. What if I caught a trout too big to flip onto shore or in a stretch of the river whose banks were steep and brushy? I decided not to go back – I was more interested in renewing my acquaintance with the river than in catching a fish.

I settled into a quiet movement with the river. It took me through a flat meadow, rich with nettle and touch-me-not and dense ivy which covered the black earth like a lush carpet. In a tall poplar a pair of handsome cedar waxwings filled the air with their clear, throaty song. The banks were cut with the deep paths of deer that came to drink in the quiet of dawn and the setting of the sun.

I moved lazily with the current which carried me out of the flat meadow and into the mystery of the woods. The water seemed darker here, more somber, subdued without the yellow sunshine of the meadow.

Now it flowed surely as the land sloped gradually downward into deeper forest. The weeds along the riverbank grew sparse, giving way to the deep, cool shade cast by towering cedars. The ground was covered with moss and the brown needles of the pine, in some places completely shaded by the thick canopy of branches that spread like a cool roof high overhead. Lying about the forest floor were huge, moss-covered logs, scattered like the giant bones of some long-forgotten species. The calls of birds echoed hollowly, as in a high-vaulted cathedral where light filtered down dimly through windows of richly-colored glass.

Moving quietly through this deep and somber forest, I suddenly felt quite lonely and forlorn, almost as if I might dissolve and float up on a shaft of sunlight and dissipate in the upper reaches of the sun. I felt a need to be busy, to occupy myself with activity, to call back my spirit from the cool shadows of the forest where it flirted with mysteries I could not fathom.

The current took me toward a bend where a giant cedar had long ago given up its struggle to stand. The river had fingered the dirt from its roots until it finally had fallen into the water, its trunk spanning the river and its branches blocking the current along the opposite bank. Not to be denied, the river had worked insidiously to free itself from the tangle of branches, forming a deep cut under and behind the top where the water swirled black and piled up yellow foam against the outer edge of the bend.

This was where the river held its richest secrets. Beneath this whorl of foam lay the most wonderful fruits the Pigeon had to offer. I cast a fly toward the upper angle of the bend, letting the line out with the current. It floated toward the deep, black water, a tiny speck of brown tied to me with the flimsiest of lifelines. I watched the fly drift closer to the turbulence beneath the branches of the cedar, feeling as if all time was suspended and the universe had slowed to watch a tiny bit of fur as it danced lightly over the water.

Suddenly a fury broke loose from out of the black. In a thrashing and an arching of energy a brown trout broke the surface, the fly imbedded in his bony jaw. The water fell from him in silver scales, and for a moment he hung weightlessly in the air before falling back into the water with writhing fury.

He disappeared into the dark water and my line whined out, hot in my fingers as I tried to slow its unwinding. The tip of my rod bent nearly double as I began to exert counter pressure on the line. For a moment it seemed I was powerless to slow the fish; he moved effortlessly and strongly away from me. Then he slowed, turned, and began to swim back toward me. I worked furiously to keep pressure on the line. Suddenly he turned and was gone again, the line screaming through the guides of the slender rod.

Once more he slowed and circled and returned, this time splitting the water and shaking himself in a show of glistening power. He broke through the water in the midst of the limbs of the cedar, and for a moment he hung there, the line caught in the feathery mesh of bare branches. My heart leaped up, held by the raw, primitive beauty of his power, loving the tie I had to him through the slender line, fearing it would break and he would be gone and I would be left alone without his magic. Then he fell back into the water, the line miraculously still attached, the bit of brown fur still imbedded in his jaw.

He began his race downstream once more, turned, returned, and sped away again, but this time with lessening power. He was tiring. He broke the water to shake his head, then fell back into it and lay motionless for a moment before he began his race downstream.

My fingers told me he had lost his fury and explosive energy and now was offering only dogged resistance. I no longer fought to keep up with his mad movements; I led him and worked him in shorter circles, feeling him tire and grow listless and lose his will.

Now I must decide what to do. Without the landing net I could not possibly take him from the water. The fragile line would never support his weight if I were to try and flip him from the water onto the bank. If only I could touch him, heft him, feel the weight of his smooth, pliant belly in my hand.

He broke the surface again, but this time he only cut it and swam with his back arching out of the water, moving in short bursts, bewildered by the force that blocked his movements. I kept the line taut, working him toward me, keeping the tip of my rod high, making him stay on top of the water.

His back was black satin tinged with light, broad and strong and muscular. As he rolled in the water I saw the scarlet and gold flecks of his sides, and a hint of his belly tinged in creamy white. I was moved by his power and grace, and I felt remorse for having caught him with my tiny bit of treachery.

He slowly swam and rolled in the water about me, and I knew, even if only for a moment, I had to touch him. I had to lay my hand on the wonderful broad back, to make a physical connection with one so rare and mysterious.

He was within reach. I brought him up in the water before me, and I slowly moved my hand up from his tail, along his back, and up to his wide, armored head. For a moment we both were motionless. The river, the forest, the sky - all ceased to be except for me and the wonderful creature which lay motionless under my hand.

Then, as if waking from a dream, he gathered himself and began to move. In a flash of energy he rose from under my hand, snapped the line with a twist of his head, and was gone beneath the black waters of the Pigeon.

I stood transfixed for a long time, letting the current tug at the line, feeling nothing but the coolness of my hand where it had lain on his back, remembering the sleek, satiny feel of his power, trying to recapture the mystery before I turned and made my way up the river to the van.

CHAPTER 12

LIFE ON WELLMAN ROAD

I never intended to fall in love with three acres of land and an old farm house with mold in the basement and mice in the attic.

Heavens knew I was done with drafty bedrooms that heated up like forges in summer and froze water in the glass on the nightstand in winter. Antiquated kitchens with worn linoleum and corroded plumbing under sinks that leaked held no promise of places where I'd like to hunker down and drop my roots. I grew up in a place like that and wanted something with a bit more zing and polish.

But my guard was down when Wayne and I signed up for a thirty-year mortgage with no clause for "Oops - I've changed my mind."

Besides, I was in love. Wayne had staked his claim on me when I was a freshman in college, and I was married before I had a chance to catch my breath. Not that I had regrets. He was a city boy who looked at me like I was some sort of hardy plant he'd never seen growing in anyone's yard back home. He knew only girls who giggled and primped and had their hair done before social events. I was a no-nonsense farm girl who thrived on adversity and hard work and faced life head-on.

However it happened, there I was, married, and moving to a farm house in the middle of nowhere with a man who didn't know the first thing about fixing anything more than a slice of toast for breakfast.

We unpacked the borrowed trailer, turned the dog loose, and had a look around. An old chicken coop stood at the back of the yard, flanked by an ancient apple tree and an enormous willow tree that fostered dreams of an exotic tree house in the imaginations of our two young daughters. Maybe after we get settled, we suggested.

To the east stood the old barn, beautifully weathered to soft gray, a loft door hanging askew revealing moldering hay from years past. The yard was overgrown with burdock and nettles, and a few yards of rusty fence sagged between us and the neighbor's cornfield. The house was tall and lanky and garbed in chalky gold aluminum siding. A rutted driveway curved out to the gravel road and clouds of dust billowed behind passing pickup trucks that rattled by.

In the weeks that followed we became acquainted with the foibles of our new home. We learned that using the toaster while the vacuum was running caused half the house to lose power. A strong northwest wind made the old metal roof whine like a tired toddler. The antiquated water softener in the basement had to be regenerated manually and took the expertise of a mechanical engineer. The septic system developed a pungency that brought tears to our eyes and led us to the realization that we lacked a drain field and the tank required pumping every three weeks.

But our new home retained its appeal in spite of its emerging warts. It was a haven of quiet serenity with privacy but not isolation. We could see the miniature cars driving down the distant highway to the south, but we could not hear their sound. Bird songs and winds sighing through trees became our rural music.

But before long, serenity and privacy grew tedious. I needed more. I needed to see gardens growing, animals grazing, fruit trees blooming. Wayne grew silent and looked helpless when I told him of my plans for our farm.

"Chickens," I said, "We need Chickens." We drove the Oldsmobile to a local egg farm where we purchased 50 white leghorns for 35 cents each. "Just a tad past their laying peak," the owner told us. "Spent," we were to find out. We shoved them into burlap grain bags, piled them in the back seat and trunk, and drove home. The 94-degree afternoon was quite bearable in the air-conditioned interior, but the trunk heated up like an oven. When we hauled the bags out of the trunk, the contents were strangely quiet. We slid the hens onto the grass in the makeshift hen yard and they stared up at us, glassy-eyed and inert. Wayne said fatalistically, "We've killed them."

"Just napping," I pronounced as I patted their cheeks, pumped their bony breasts up and down, and blew air into their beaks. A few stirred, flopped around, and made strange chicken sounds in their scrawny throats. Others twitched convulsively, lurched about, then gave up the ghost, settling into little heaps of dusty yellowed feathers.

"Quick," I said, "Off with their heads and we'll have meat for the freezer." We left the living with water and grain and set about plucking the fallen. Their chests and legs were mainly bones with a few stringy muscles holding things together. "Stewing hens," I muttered, beginning to lose my enthusiasm.

Later, returning to the chicken pen, Wayne observed, "The girls are all lying down; what's the matter?"

"Just resting," I decided. I lifted the nearest hen to her feet and steered her toward the grain pan. She stumbled forward, fell on her face, and lay there with bony tail turned up to the sun. "Odd," I muttered. I soon learned my cage-grown hens had no idea what the good earth was for nor how to walk on it. In fact, they seemed to be genuinely terrified of this strange new world.

For the next few days they eyed their surroundings in dull fear, driven only by sheer thirst and hunger to discover how their legs worked. But when they figured it out, they blossomed into creatures that suddenly had discovered the Promised Land. They joyfully gained their strength, plumped up their scrawny bodies, and began shucking out eggs at a remarkable rate. Wayne said it was pure gratitude for being rescued from their concentration-camp cages where there was no room to move about. At any rate, they sang cheerful chicken songs, laid eggs in abundance, scratched the chicken yard into a virtual dust bowl for several years, finally dying contentedly from old age. Their "meat for the freezer" counterparts were eventually buried in a common grave, their carcasses so tough and stringy that no amount of simmering made them edible.

Wayne's gentle nature recovered nicely from rehabilitating spent hens, and he decided to incubate eggs and build his flock from scratch. I, daughter of a poor dirt farmer, assumed he would poke a dozen or so fertile eggs under a setting hen and let nature take its course. But he, son of a well-heeled city family, amassed catalogs and brochures, then sent away for large electric incubators and fertile eggs of exotic breeds packed in excelsior.

He quickly and gleefully entered his incubation phase. The basement became his field of dreams, and he turned, sprinkled, and arranged the eggs according to the rules set forth in the pamphlets he pored over.

When the first chick pipped a small hole in its shell, Wayne swelled with paternal awe and pride. One by one the tiny creatures emerged, their wet down drying to soft fluff. From all sizes and colors of eggs came Buff Cochin, Silkie, Polish Crested, Aracauna, and Rhode Island Red chickens, Bronze and White Turkeys, Kahki Campbell, Indian Runner, Muscovy, and Pekin ducks, Guinea fowl, and long-necked Pilgrim and White Chinese geese.

Quickly outgrowing the incubators, the chicks were moved into larger brooders in the living room. Cheerful, noisy creatures ate mash and napped under heat lights.

"They will need more spacious housing," I told Wayne after they doubled in size in mere days. So from the living room they were relocated to makeshift pens hastily constructed in the back yard. They grew at a remarkable rate, as did our grain bill at the local elevator. Eventually we took down the fences and gave them free run of the three acres, where they avidly devoured the spring strawberry crop, ate rows of lettuce and beans, and left craters scratched in the garden where they dusted themselves and lounged in the sun.

They rewarded us with an abundance of eggs of all colors and sizes - soft beige, white, brown speckled, olive green and soft pink. The Kahki Campbell ducks laid their eggs in the yard, dropping them at random and making each morning an Easter egg hunt for our daughters.

During this heady time of homesteading we discovered Mother Earth, a magazine that opened our eyes to the wonders of living off the land. Soon the old barn groaned with new life. Three Nubian goats munched alfalfa in the front pen and waited placidly to be milked. A Holstein steer grew fat in the side yard. Two welch ponies kept the pasture nibbled down to the earth.

Our monthly magazine instructed us in mulching, composting, root cellaring, preserving, and propagating.

Our days were spent working like inspired field hands under the Michigan sun, and our evenings were spent dreaming of new projects for the coming days.

One article grabbed our attention. Raising hogs on elevated pens. Wow, I thought. No smelly hog yards like the ones on my childhood farm. No toting buckets of messy slop to pour into troughs lined by noisy, ravenous pigs. Just a tidy platform with one-inch spaces between the floor boards, a neat fence around the perimeter, a convenient three-foot space between the floor and the earth below. The theory, as I remember, was that the pigs lounged on their raised living room, nibbled on their rations, and any unpleasant debris fell through the cracks in the floor to be shoveled into a tidy pile nearby.

We hauled armfuls of sweet corn stalks and pitched them over the walls, flung in baskets of overgrown zucchini and overripe tomatoes, and listened to the satisfied smacking of three hogs that grew fatter by the day. The problem with our system became apparent when the debris failed to fall neatly through the cracks in the floor, and nothing collected on the ground to be shoveled away. Instead the floor gradually disappeared beneath a tangle of vegetation, corn cobs, and hog manure. The air grew ripe with the smell of hogs confined in a small space clogged with composting vegetation.

We gradually abandoned the dream of a tidy pen of immaculate hogs lounging on their air-cooled platform. Instead we held our noses and doggedly pitched in as much food as our crusty captives could consume, counting the days until market time. Then we herded them down a makeshift ramp into a trailer and sent them off to the local processing plant. No more hogs, Wayne said. He claimed to prefer oatmeal to bacon anyway.

We gravitated away from large animals after the hog fiasco. Our conviction that smaller was better was reinforced by the Holstein steer which grew lanky and tall in his end of the barn. He became somewhat sullen about his confinement and responded by repeatedly kicking backward with both feet, making craters in the walls. We would gladly have let him out to enjoy the great outdoors, but our sagging fences would never have confined him and he'd have fled to parts unknown at the first taste of freedom. So we ignored the echoing booms and counted the days until he was big enough to butcher.

We tried valiantly to become self-sustaining and grow our own food. Rabbits grew plump in wire cages and awaited their destiny as dinner. A goat kid was fattened on grain and I contemplated creative ways to serve chevon. A turkey strutted down the driveway in full regalia, his breast growing more plump as Thanksgiving approached. But something tugged at my heart as I tended to our growing menagerie. We gave names to our feathered and furry friends that reminded us of people we loved. The old gray geese were named Hattie and Alfred after my grandparents. An irascible old doe became Ethyl, the eccentric aunt who slept in a bed suspended from the ceiling with ropes to protect her from night vapors. The rabbits were Peter and Thumper and Molly and George. Our appetite for meat lessened as each candidate for our dinner endeared itself to our hearts.

Eventually we adopted a lifestyle that moved toward vegetarianism. When we were hungry for steaks we dined out, preferring not to know our main course on a first name basis. Our menus at home favored milk and cheese from our herd of goats, eggs from the coop, and vegetable casseroles from the garden. Our favored reading material gradually shifted from Mother Earth and its occasional carnivorous theme to seed catalogs that appealed to our more benign appetites.

One cold winter's night in January I sat curled up under a flannel blanket thumbing through a stack of seed catalogs. The glossy pages were filled with visions of creamy white cauliflower, plump ears of golden sweet corn, crimson tomatoes bursting with flavor, flowers of every hue of the rainbow, fruit trees heavy with perfect delights for the tasting - but oh, the nut trees! These tall giants towering above the rest drew me in with their promise of bushels of plump nuts, crisp and succulent, growing faithfully year after year.

I was hooked. I turned to the "order now" page and committed my soul to two Carpathian walnut trees, to be delivered at the "appropriate planting time for your area." I wrote the check and waited impatiently for spring.

Then one day the following April during a sleet storm my trees arrived. Plant immediately, the packing slip said. I apologetically stored them in our cool basement and promised them a proper planting the minute the weather cleared. A week later I donned boots and a parka, grabbed the shovel, and scouted the yard for favorable planting sites. One tree would go to the east of the house, the other nearby on the other side of the driveway.

I dug the holes, unwrapped the trees, and read the final directions. Form a loose crumbly base at the bottom of the hole, fan the roots out, and place over the base. Fill the hole with soil, tamping firmly around the trunk. I looked dismally at the pile of mud beside the hole and shoveled in a few soggy lumps. Icy water oozed up and puddled at the base of the spindly trunks when the planting was complete, and I mentally apologized for the rude beginning and retreated to the house.

A few weeks later, when I could bear to look in the direction of my new trees, I was astounded to see delicate pale green leaves feathering the branches. They lived! As spring settled in the trees prospered, adding height weekly.

Then in early June Wayne came into the kitchen looking stricken. "There has been a slight accident involving one of your nut trees," he murmured guiltily. "I backed over it with the pickup." I rushed outside to find it snapped off six inches above the ground. Only Wayne's obvious remorse kept me from grabbing the severed tree and thrashing him with it.

"I still have the other tree across the driveway," I muttered with forced charity.

The remaining tree, as if sensing the pressure as sole survivor, grew at a remarkable rate. By mid-summer it was full and lush, standing nearly as tall as me. Then one day Wayne came into the kitchen with that familiar look on his face. "Uh, there has been a slight problem with your nut tree," he announced forlornly. "A couple of goats got out and sort of trimmed it." I knew very well that goats do not "sort of" trim anything. They gleefully and voraciously devour vegetation at an astounding rate. I raced to the yard to find my tree denuded of leaves and most of its branches. Its stocky trunk rose forlornly above goat hoof prints in the soil below. My heart sank. No more dreams of bushels of plump nuts growing faithfully year after year.

The following Sunday I stood before my Sunday school class of six-year-olds. The lesson involved prayer, and the children discussed the things they needed divine help with. At the conclusion one child said, "Mrs. Brown, what do you need to pray about?"

"My nut tree," I answered impulsively. "The goats ate it and I think they killed it." The sweet prayers that followed included requests to "please make Mrs. Brown's tree live." I apologized to God on the way home from church for putting Him on the spot like that.

For weeks I averted my eyes when I walked past the stub. Then one day I accidentally glanced in its direction. The tree lived! Not only did it live, it burst forth with new growth and stood covered in lush green leaves. The tree really did grow to towering heights and produced bushels of plump nuts year after year. I still feel a special warmth as I gather the harvest each fall.

Wayne and I still live on our beloved three acres, among the gentle ghosts of the creatures we came to love. The children left home to begin their own adventures, and our gardens gravitated away from potatoes and corn and toward zinnias and lavender. The animals gradually expired from old age and the barn fell into disrepair. With sadness we watched our local fire department as they burned it in a training session one still autumn evening.

Life has been good on our three acres. Wayne and I have grown old here. We have felt the gentle flow of nature carry us through the years and we have watched the seasons bring life and change and death with comforting regularity. I wouldn't have changed it for the world.

CHAPTER 13

OATMEAL THE GOAT

If it hadn't been for Jamie we would never have become goat farmers. Practically from birth she had been plagued with allergic ailments that necessitated special diets, a shoe box full of soothing ointments, and visits to specialists who endured her weeping fits as she clutched my neck and begged to go home.

When we bought our country home in 1972 it seemed only logical to throw ourselves into the organic movement, eliminate nasty chemicals in our food, buy a couple of Nubian goats, and turn Jamie into a healthy kid who no longer itched, wheezed, or peered at the world through swollen, red-rimmed eyes.

Our weathered, gray barn was shoveled out, spruced up, and divided into pens to welcome three Nubian does who eyed us and their new surroundings with mild suspicion. They were quickly won over by Kari who secretly fed them Twinkies and cheese crackers, and they joined our family with enthusiasm.

Gretchen, sway-backed and bony, was the herd queen, and she ruled with a vengeance. Pebbles, long-haired and dingy white, patiently endured Gretchen's sour temper and maintained her cheerful outlook admirably. Lois, the third resident, was oblivious to anything but food and the attention of humans. The three of them sunned on the cement pad outside the barn, the remains of a silo that had once stood there in years past. We hauled in an old claw-foot bath tub and some large climbing rocks, and the pad became their favorite spot to lounge and cavort.

They quickly taught us the basics of goat husbandry. With their haughty roman noses held high, they rejected any food but alfalfa hay, preferably third cutting, served in a dry, tidy manger, never on the ground. Fresh-cut tree trimmings were acceptable, willow and apple the most desirable, and nettles were ambrosia to their delicate taste buds. Grain at milking time could never be dusty; it must be lightly moistened with molasses and just a touch of mineral salt. Grass was to walk on and prevent mud puddles after rainstorms; it was not acceptable food unless it was the only alternative to starvation.

I became the resident milk maid, a job I loved. Untethered and standing outside in the barnyard, my does stood placidly and munched their grain while I squatted and milked them. I would bury my head in their sweet-smelling flank and watch as the streams of pure white milk created a lovely froth in my shiny new bucket.

Summer merged into autumn, then winter. My does cared nothing about the vagaries of Michigan climate; whether sun, rain, or bitter cold, they needed fresh water, clean bedding, and a diet that pleased them. But their delight in my presence, and their unabashed affection for me and my family made caring for them more joy than duty, and milking them twice daily more than compensated for a little sleet in my face or mud sloshing underfoot.

My books from Rodale Press, the authority on living off the land, told me that I must have the does bred, then stop milking a few months before kidding season in the spring. A call to a seasoned goat farmer nearby resulted in the appearance of Royal Viking Ragnar, a muscular black goat with fire in his eyes. He seemed to relish his visit in the goat yard, and the does were shamelessly wooed by him. He nuzzled and groomed each one in her turn, and she became smitten by his virile charms.

Kari and Jamie, urban children until just recently, were afforded a frank and vivid picture of the beginnings of life on the farm. They asked many questions during the mating season, and their wide eyes reflected the earthy wonder of procreation.

After Ragnar was returned to his own barnyard, the does having settled into motherhood and wanting little to do with his pungent presence, life returned to normal. We watched with delight as their abdomens swelled in the months that followed, and we looked forward to kidding time.

In early March the miracle happened. Within days, six kids made their appearance, three from Pebbles, two from Gretchen, and one from Lois. They were beautiful beyond words. Long, silken ears that hung to their shoulders, straight, long legs that seemed to contain springs as they bounded and leaped into the air from sheer joy, soft coats dappled with black and brown and gray - we fell hopelessly in love with them.

As the kids grew the pens seemed to shrink. The does, especially Gretchen, grew cranky at the boisterous newcomers that leaped and bounced on anything available, even a sleeping mother. We began to realize that these wonderful creatures were not toys but livestock that required management and planning. The kids, five does and one buck, would need to be disbudded, a procedure that removed the beginning of horns, a danger to the herd if left to grow unchecked.

I became the practical manager of the herd, Wayne using his city upbringing as a reason not to deal with unpleasant realities, and the girls too tender-hearted to even consider anything more than cuddling and cavorting with the goats. So one Monday morning I herded the six kids into our old Dodge van and headed for the local Vet's to have the horn buds removed. Before arriving at the Vet's, I stopped on Main Street and made a quick visit to our local bank. The van was angle parked in front, and I left the untethered kids with instructions to behave themselves. When I came out of the bank I saw a group of people standing in front of the van, pointing and chuckling. There in the front window, feet up on the dash board and long, velvet ears dangling, stood six little goats, staring back at the admirers and making happy little bleating noises in greeting.

The next stop dampened their spirits a bit. Our vet, a soft-hearted woman with a deep love for her patients, apologized to the kids as she held a red-hot disbudding iron over each bud until the hair was burned away and a ring of charred tissue remained. They, having never experienced anything more painful than a head butt to their backside by an impatient doe, were beside themselves with horror as they shook their heads to try to escape the pain.

The ride home was subdued, with the kids clustered in the back corner, heads down and bleating pathetically. I told myself that what I had done was necessary, but I felt like a heartless brute who had deliberately inflicted pain on innocent babies. I began to realize that all was not hearts and flowers where raising animals was concerned.

The kids recovered and forgot the ordeal faster than I did. They held no grudges, and I was once more greeted with joy and affection when I entered the goat yard. I shamelessly bought favor with them by bringing sweet treats and apple slices, and the past was quickly forgiven.

Our next unpleasant decision regarded the single male kid, a stocky replica of his father, but with long, mottled gray hair like his mother Pebbles. Only registered male kids are allowed to grow up to become bucks for breeding, declared my dairy goat journal. All others are neutered and used as pets or food. Once again the role of rational, cold-hearted manager of the herd fell to me. I announced that this single male would be neutered and would become food for the table when he reached his full growth.

The girls and Wayne were horrified. In wide-eyed wonder they decided that my plan was totally unacceptable, and they would just as soon eat each other as this sweet, furry little fellow nuzzling their hands for treats. I put them off with "we'll talk about it later," and went about my business.

Shortly thereafter I said casually to the girls, "This little fellow is the color of a bowl of oatmeal. Say, that would be a great name! Let's call him 'Oatmeal.'" My plan, which I thought was subtle and brilliant, was to introduce the idea of food into our references to the male kid, now named after something that showed up on the table at meal time. They eyed me suspiciously, but I smiled innocently even though in my heart I felt like a cold traitor.

Summer passed pleasantly. The goats basked in the sun and romped with each other and Jamie and Kari who spent hours in the barn yard with them. We learned much as we managed the herd and accustomed ourselves to the personalities of our four-footed family members. Gretchen continued to be the cranky boss of the herd, and she took pleasure in knocking her subjects out of her way when she pleased. Lois was happily neutral, unfazed by anything and showing no interest in grabbing the spotlight. Pebbles was the one that captured my heart.

She always walked beside me when I entered the barnyard, and she had an uncanny ability to sense my mood and reflect it in her behavior. If I was sad, she nuzzled me gently. If I was impatient and in a hurry, she stayed out of my path and became business-like herself. If I was filled with delight she would bounce like a young kid, her generous udder swinging like a silken pendulum.

One day I was pitching hay into the area in front of the mangers, and Jamie was climbing into the pen to play with the kids. She stumbled and fell against the wall, and a protruding nail gouged a bloody line in her hand. Her cries made me drop my pitchfork and bolt over the face of the manger to tend to her. But before I could reach her, Pebbles moved gently to her side and began to nuzzle and lick her, much the same way she would behave toward one of her own kids. I watched in wonder as Jamie stopped crying and accepted Pebbles' comfort and gentle attention. This remarkable creature showed mothering instincts that were very much like my own.

Autumn flooded our world with golden sunshine. The girls were back in school, and I reveled in long days of puttering in the perennial gardens and harvesting remnants of summer vegetables. One afternoon I had occasion to visit the goat barn, and, as I always did, I took a mental head count of the herd. Eight. I counted again. There should be nine. Eight again. Someone was missing. I quickly determined that Oatmeal was the missing member.

"Oatmeal?" I called. A faint bleat seemed to be coming from within the wall. I called again. Again I heard the faint answer. The other goats and I craned our necks and looked in every possible cranny where a goat could hide. In one corner of the pen stood an old horse manger, a v-shaped relic of previous owners and their livestock. Above the end opposite the corner was a slanted crawl space that sloped from the ceiling to the wall below making a triangular tunnel that ended twenty feet away at the opposite wall. I had never paid much attention to this mystery tunnel seven feet above my head, finding no purpose for its existence. It seemed to be just a whimsical remnant of some long-forgotten function of early farming.

I crawled up into the horse manger, stood on the open end, peered into the dark tunnel and called Oatmeal's name. Another soft bleat, this time closer.

I made a quick trip to the house and back with a flashlight and once more climbed into the horse manger. Standing on tip-toe, I peered down the long tunnel, the light beam revealing decades of chaff, cobwebs, and, at the far end, two eyes that gleamed in the reflection of the light.

"For Pete's sake, Oatmeal, how did you get yourself in this mess?" I asked pointlessly. I crawled into the tunnel and wriggled my way toward the end. When I reached Oatmeal I grasped him by his neck and pulled, expecting him to follow me as I tried to back up. Nothing. He grunted and thrashed a bit, but he didn't budge. I pulled as hard as I could in such cramped quarters, but it soon became obvious that he was securely lodged.

I backed my way out of the tunnel and contemplated my next move. The only possible access to my trapped goat seemed to be from above. I climbed a makeshift ladder made of narrow boards that were nailed to the side of the wall. It led to a square opening overhead, the only access to the floor above.

The hay mow was a desolate place that housed a flock of pigeons and an occasional mouse. The floor was covered in old hay, weathered boards, and a few old hay forks with broken handles. I made my way to the back corner under which, I assumed, was oatmeal. Using the tines of a rusty fork, I scraped and dug my way to the floor. The boards were loose and came up easily with a bit of tugging.

As I enlarged the hole in the floor I could see a bit of gray hair below, and an enthusiastic bleat let me know that Oatmeal was delighted to see both daylight and me. When the last board blocking my access to him was removed, I could see what was keeping him prisoner. He had apparently crawled into the tunnel above the manager, and for some reason had begun backing up. The further he backed, the narrower the opening became, and he had finally come to the end where a huge, hand-hewn beam blocked any more movement. He must have wriggled about, wedging his spine further under the beam, until he was unable to move any more.

With much tugging, grunting, and digging the straw from beneath him, I finally freed him and he clambered up into the hay mow. He was genuinely pleased to see me, and his recent misery was quickly replaced with a curiosity about his new surroundings. While he explored I pondered how I was going to get him down from the hay mow. The only access to the world below was the square hole with the descending ladder which I had climbed, and a small door that opened to the outside, with a fifteen-foot drop to the ground below.

The only possibility was the hole in the floor. It was unlikely that I could persuade Oatmeal to climb down the vertical ladder; I had to come up with a more plausible plan. The only solution seemed to be a sort of truss made of ropes with which I could lower him to the first floor. Having never made a rope truss before, I tried to visualize just how one would work.

I obviously needed ropes. I climbed down the ladder and headed to the garage for equipment. After digging through boxes of things which were mainly useless but which were too good to throw away, I came upon some old clothesline rope, a section of water ski rope, some binder twine, and a coil of old hay rope. Surely I could make do with such a diverse collection.

Back to the hay mow I went, the goats standing in a ring below the opening in the floor and looking up in wonder. Oatmeal was most interested in the material I had brought with me, and watched with interest as I made two loops with the clothesline rope, one behind his front legs and the other in front of his hind legs. I tied the two loops together above his back and gave an upward tug to test my handiwork. The front loop slid to the rear, and he was left balancing on his front legs with his rear end suspended in the air behind him.

My second attempt seemed more logical. Using separate ropes for the front and back loops, I pulled upward. This time all four of his feet were raised an equal distance above the hay floor. I joined the two ropes to a long section of hay rope, one which would safely lower

him to the pen below. I left enough slack to slow his descent to a few feet from the first floor and wrapped the
remainder around my waist.

"All right, Oatmeal," I announced, "Let's get you back
where you belong." He looked at me with bland disin-
terest and stood his ground. I pushed him toward the
opening and he set all four feet and dug in. I grabbed
his back legs and pushed them toward the hole. He
spraddled his front legs out and braced himself. I tried
the same tactic with his front legs and his back legs shot
out and braced himself from the other end. I tried to
encircle all four legs and stuff him down the hole and
he thrashed and fought until I let go.

Down below the herd murmured and gazed up at us
with interest.

Once more I tried to capture all four legs and push
him toward the hole. Still no success. Taking a length
of binder twine, I made a loop and managed to maneu-
ver him into stepping into the circle. I quickly pulled it
tight and trussed up his legs. Now I had him! With a
grunt I pushed him into the opening and he shot downward. I saw a brief image of a circle of upturned faces
watching one of their own hurtling at them from above,
bleating frantically. I barely had time to grab the rope

tied around my waist and fling myself backward, slowing his descent before he hit the floor below.

With relief I climbed down the ladder and untied Oatmeal and then myself. He moved away from me and ignored my apologies for handling him so roughly. It took an apple and an Oreo cookie to restore his good humor and mend our fractured friendship.

Time passed and the day inevitably arrived when Oatmeal's fate must be decided. The family was sharply divided regarding that fate. The girls could barely talk about changing him from a barnyard inhabitant to chevon, while I bravely supported the practical theory that farm animals, however engaging they may be, must carry their weight in the grand scheme of things, even though that meant that some were destined to be eaten. Wayne rode the fence, agreeing with me in principle, but siding with the girls when he listened to his tender heart.

Practicality won out. Oatmeal was sent to the local meat processing plant where he was converted into small white packages with labels like "chops" and "roast" and "ground chevon." I waited for a few weeks before I brought a package up from the freezer in the basement and steeled myself to prepare my first meal of chevon.

What followed remains a blur in my memory. I remember faces at the table changing from happy expectation to disbelief as they found out the main course. I recall a few feeble attempts to sample tiny chops beneath the disguise of sliced onions and mushroom sauce. I see tear-filled eyes and hear reasons why vegetables and bread are all the diners care for.

I was forced to face reality. Our goats were too much like members of the family to become food for our table. They had captured our hearts, and we loved them too much to let cold reason rule their fate.

Weeks passed before I could bear to think about the grocery sack filled with small white packages tucked away in the freezer. Then one day when the sun was shining and my heart had nearly healed, I dug a deep hole under the apple tree in the back yard. I brought the sack of chevon up from the basement and carried it to its final destination. As I unwrapped each package and laid the contents in the hole, I promised myself that I would never again be ruled by cold reason alone. Sometimes the impractical must be accepted. Logic is necessary, but so is love.

CHAPTER 14

ANGELS I HAVE KNOWN

There are wonders in life that we cannot see. The beauty that abounds in the depths of the ocean is painted in hues that only our minds can imagine. The unseen world that moves silently under the grass of a meadow is invisible to us as we stroll on Sunday walks. The miraculous life that pulsates in our own bodies can only be sensed as we move through our days.

We watch the world unfold through eyes that struggle to see logic and order and just cause. We face our realities with hopeful vigor when the light is strong, and stoic determination when darkness covers us. Sometimes we fall into chasms of desolation and cry for our mothers or magic or God. And sometimes those cries are answered.

In my lifetime I have been given glimpses of those answers that cannot be explained by logic and natural cause. Some have been dramatic and profound, others gentle and simple. But all have led me to believe that above and around us live an invisible host of angelic beings that touch our lives in ways we rarely see. Mostly we go through our days unscathed by crisis or danger or tragedy. But when such wrenching moments explode in our private worlds, we are sometimes aided and rescued by strangers that can only be explained as angelic.

My first awareness of angels came from a conversation I had with an elderly aunt many years ago. I was terribly young and sophisticated and cynical about all things not firmly rooted in science, and her gentle words were received with polite incredulity. I attributed her account to indigestion or a chemical reaction to medication.

She recalled a recent afternoon when she was sitting in her favorite chair crocheting doilies for the church bazaar. Her arthritic fingers struggled with the stitches, and she concentrated fully on keeping the loops even and taut. As she worked she became aware of a presence in her tiny apartment. She was not afraid, only curious. She looked toward the door, and the sweep of her first glance began at the threshold. There she saw the feet of a large man standing motionless. He was wearing sandals of gold rope and a robe of white that came nearly to the top of his feet. Her eyes slowly swept upward and she saw a yellow rope looped loosely around his waist and knotted at one side. At each side of his waist she saw large hands held with the palms toward her as if waiting to embrace her.

At this point I asked her if she could have been dreaming. She said she was certain she was awake and that all the details in the room were normal and un-remarkable. She returned to her story, telling me that she continued to look at the man in her doorway with curiosity. Her eyes swept upward toward his face, and she saw the smooth strength of his neck and jaw. She told me at this point she believed he was an angel come to take her to heaven. Her ninety-eight years of life had been spent with the quiet underlying confidence that heaven awaited her when she died, and she thought that moment had come. But just as her eyes looked toward his, he disappeared. She sat quietly and pensively for a moment, then she said, "I was so disappointed. I thought I was finally going to get to go home, and with such a handsome escort. But I guess my time had not yet come."

I smiled as I hugged her frail shoulders and left, thinking that she had imagined a pleasant encounter with a figure conjured up from a Sunday school lesson in her youth. Today I am not so sure. I believe she really was visited by a gentle angel who appeared with the sole purpose of bringing her comfort and reassurance of her future.

Ministering angels may not always be visible. I believe that they frequently move about us and help us in ways both life-changing and minute. I was recently driving home from an appointment and I was exhausted and sleepy. I forced myself to stay alert, but as I neared my destination I let down my guard. A mile from home I was jolted awake and I saw a semi-truck directly in my path and feet away. I had fallen asleep and drifted into the oncoming lane. My steering wheel was wrenched to the right by invisible hands and the truck flew by, missing me by inches. It was with profound gratitude that I thanked God for sending an angel to rescue me from certain death.

Sometimes we are helped in small ways that bless us like a gentle hug from a good friend. My daughter Jamie called me one day and asked me if I had a used humidifier in my attic. She was in need of one and I told her she was welcome to mine. When I had stored it several years before, I had first cleaned it and put the working parts, including the detachable electric cord, inside the reservoir. When I retrieved it from the attic I was frustrated to find the cord missing. I looked in all the obvious places, searched the unlikely spots, then began rifling through crannies which my common sense told me could not possibly yield the missing item. With growing annoyance I determined that the cord was gone.

I decided to give the humidifier to my daughter as it was, thinking she could either find a replacement cord, or else put it out with the trash. As I brushed my teeth just before I was to leave for Jamie's, I breathed a brief prayer; "God, wherever did I leave that cord?"

Immediately a voice spoke in my mind saying, "Look in the right hand drawer in the dining room desk." I knew the contents of that drawer. It was tiny and held only small bits of paper and stickers for my grandchildren's art projects. I politely answered the voice, "I'll look when I finish brushing my teeth."

I heard, "If you wait it won't be there." So dribbling bubbles down my chin I hurried to the desk, pulled open the drawer, and there on top was the missing cord. I had opened that drawer many times in the preceding months, and I knew the drawer held only children's art work. I felt a joyful warmth as I realized that I had undoubtedly been visited by a heavenly being who did the bidding of a heavenly father who cares about his children even in the smallest of ways.

A quiet joy in my life has been the assurance that my daughter Kari and her children have a veritable army of angels that attend them. It is comfort indeed when I think of their life style. My five grandchildren have been raised to believe there are no limits on what they can explore and achieve. They are fearless, creative, and adventuresome. They have grown up with a deep faith in the power of prayer, and they are often called upon to intercede when others face trouble.

A family friend, a sheriff's deputy, called one snowy winter day to ask the kids to pray for him. The previous evening he had returned to his car from a visit to K-Mart and was preoccupied with the heavy snowfall and the driving difficulty it created. When he arrived home he discovered to his horror that he had dropped a ring of keys that opened every door of the Sheriff's department building. He drove back to the K-Mart parking lot and found snow piled in small mountains as heavy equipment cleaned up the storm's aftermath. There was no sign of the missing keys.

Early the next morning he called Kari and asked her family to pray for him. They all quickly asked God to help him find his keys. He drove back to the parking lot, got out near a pile of snow, reached into the base and felt the icy metal of the key ring in his hand. When he looked at the number of snowy heaps and considered the unlikelihood of finding the keys at first try he knew it was more than coincidence; he had been blessed with a speedy answer to prayer, perhaps assisted by an angel who tucked the keys safely out of sight and then led him to the spot where they lay.

During a similar snowy day Kari was driving her van with the children in the back. She is notorious for her checkered driving record, being not entirely reckless but certainly accident prone. She hit black ice and the van spun wildly out of control. It turned a complete circle and slid up an embankment and turned on its side, moving toward trees ahead. Simultaneously Kari shouted, "Pray, kids!" As if in slow motion the van righted itself and came down heavily on all four tires in the middle of the road. As the children announced, "That was fun, Mom," she turned the key and the stalled van came to life and proceeded as if nothing had happened. I can only imagine the angels standing in the road behind them as they continued on their way.

Sometimes angels intervene in moments when a life hangs in the balance. Such a moment occurred years ago when Kari's older boys, Christian and Isaac, were four and three. The family was spending a week in their remote cabin in Michigan's Upper Peninsula. Its total isolation and lack of lights, water, and phone suited their pioneer spirits well. Early in the week Kari's husband

Chris was cutting brush to make a small clearing outside the cabin door. He piled it in an enormous heap, adding a few small dead trees that had fallen during the previous winter.

He lit the pile and the fire blazed to life. He continued to throw brush onto the fire, but the intensity of the heat drove him back from the perimeter and he waited for the blaze to die down. The two boys played near their mother, imagining themselves firemen armed with hoses aimed at the fire. They ran about, shooting imaginary streams of water into the air, eyes sparkling with excitement.

Christian ran toward the blaze and Kari started to shout a warning to him that he was too close. Before she could get the words out Isaac, running close behind his brother, stumbled and pitched forward, his arms outstretched to break his fall. His hands hit Christian in the back and Christian was propelled into the fire. His parents could only watch in horror as he was swallowed up in the heat and flame. At that exact moment he was flung violently backward and he landed ten feet away from the blaze. It was as if a force had stopped his forward motion and thrown him clear of danger. Kari rushed to him, expecting to see him writhing in pain from critical burns. Instead he lay there breathless but unhurt. Not even his hair was singed, and he showed no evidence of the previous moment that should have ended his life. Kari could only hold him tightly and thank God for the miracle of his rescue. She was spared the unspeakable pain of having her child die before her eyes and her heart was filled with gratitude.

Years later I was visiting my sister Sally in Charleston, South Carolina. I arrived late in the day, and as I went to bed that night I looked forward to spending a week in a beautiful city with people I loved. Just before midnight I heard the phone ring and Sally came into my room looking grave. It was my husband calling from Michigan with the awful news that our son-in-law Chris had been killed in a motorcycle accident. I was overwhelmed with sadness, especially for Kari and their five children. In a moment our world had been turned upside down. Suddenly plans for sightseeing and shopping and relaxing became trivial and irrelevant. My first thought was to return to Michigan and be with my family.

Early the next morning I called the airline and explained my need to return home. The agent explained the terms of my ticket and told me it would cost me several hundred dollars to change my travel plans. I explained the tragic emergency and pleaded with him to accommodate me. Finally he arranged for a return flight for $50 and told me my ticket would be waiting for me at the airport.

I arrived at the terminal and found a throng of people struggling to make connections with a system that was not working well. I waited in line to check in electronically, and when I reached the front of the line the computer screen would not recognize my clearance. I looked for an agent, but few were available, and those who were had long lines of people waiting for help. I fought the urge to cry and I prayed for help. The next moment I heard a voice asking if I needed assistance. Amid a chorus of "Hey, I was here first!" from angry passengers I explained my situation. She said, "Wait here - I'll be right back," and disappeared behind the counter. Minutes later she reappeared with boarding passes and thrust them in my hand. She hugged me and said softly, "There is no charge. God bless you." I boarded the plane with a sense of comfort and calm in the midst of great calamity, knowing that the woman was an agent of a loving heavenly father.

Years later Kari and her children, having learned to get on with their lives, visited an aunt in El Salvador. While they were there they spent a day at a remote beach on the ocean. Late in the day as they were getting ready to leave, Levi, the youngest of the five, asked if anyone would go for one last swim with him. When no one volunteered, Kari said she would join him. They swam out farther than Kari's common sense dictated, and just as she was about to suggest they return to shore she realized that they were in a strong rip tide. Both being strong swimmers, they tried to get free of the current but could not. Levi tired quickly and began to sink beneath the water, struggling to rise again and again for breath. A friend on shore tried to swim out to them to help but had to return to shore because of the danger to himself.

Kari realized with horror that she and her son were about to drown. She shouted a prayer to the heavens saying, "God, we need help right now. My children have just lost their father, and now they are going to watch as their Mother and little brother drown. This is just not acceptable!" At that moment they saw a small Salvadoran man approach them on a boogie board. Saying nothing, he pulled Levi onto the board and paddled to shore. Then he swam back out to Kari, reached out his hand toward her, and as she took it she felt herself being propelled through the water. Almost effortlessly they glided to shore and she fell on the sand, exhausted. In the chaos that followed Kari turned to thank the young man who had saved their lives. There was no one there - only an empty beach that showed no evidence of their rescuer. Another angel graciously rescued my daughter and grandson.

In moments of grave danger or in placid stretches of tranquility God promises to be with us. When we call out to him in the face of trouble he knows what is best for us and responds to our cry. Sometimes he allows us to struggle and find our own way. Sometimes he leads us to others who can help us in our difficulty. Sometimes he sends his heavenly hosts to miraculously rescue us from certain destruction. When we are told not to worry it is for good reason; it is unnecessary and pointless when we are given the promise that "He shall give his angels charge over thee to keep thee in all thy ways."

CHAPTER 15

MY WAR WITH MOTHER NATURE

I have had it with Mother Nature and her hairy hench-men. She and her four-footed little accomplices have pushed me beyond the limit of my endurance.

This has never happened before. I have, in the past, endured blistering heat that parched the fields and shriveled the crops, weeks of driving rain that washed out roads and flooded my basement, snow that piled up to the window sills and clogged the driveway, wind-storms that toppled trees and interrupted electricity for days, hailstones the size of golf balls, the threat of torna-does embedded in towering thunder clouds – all these natural phenomena have come and gone, part of the natural cycle of life.

This year, however, has been different. Not only have I been subject to erratic temperatures, inadequate rainfall, and relentless wind, I have been assaulted by a hoard of varmints that have declared war on my little world and are apparently bent on driving me crazy. They are dangerously close to that end.

Don't get me wrong, I take pests and pestilence in stride and react with equanimity, for the most part. Cabbage loopers, tomato blight, slugs, aphids, potato beetles, damp rot - these problems generally come one or two at a time and pick a small target, leaving enough gardening endeavors alone so that I can forgive and forget. But suddenly the perfect horticultural storm has gathered over my three acres and unleashed bedlam.

It began in May. Instead of balmy spring days and pleasant nights we endured frost, snow, wintery winds, and gray skies. Cold rains drenched the land, and farmers despaired of getting corn planted before the middle of June. Lawns and weedy expanses reveled in the cool, wet weather and shot up to mid-calf and clogged mower decks with green compost. At least my raspberry patch was thriving, I thought. The sturdy shoots were covered in blossoms and promised a bountiful July harvest.

I groomed perennial gardens and mulched foundation plantings and dreamed of pots of cheerful annuals and lush tomato plants heavy with heirloom beauties.

Then as if a switch had been turned on, the temperature shot up to August oppressiveness and the rain fled for other parts of the country where it fell in abundance and flooded the poor folks in its path. We were left with sweltering days shrouded in clouds of dust driven by constant wind.

Then, along with these indignities of nature that tried our mettle, the local animal kingdom got up in arms and turned on us. The moles were first. They began by crisscrossing the grass with tunnels that erupted into mounds of dirt like little volcanoes. As the dry spell progressed, the grass above the tunnels shriveled and turned brown, leaving erratic paths of desolation.

Then the chipmunks went crazy. They moved into our yard and threw themselves into tunneling and mining the ground around the house until my gardens looked like Swiss cheese. Not content to set up underground cities where they might raise their young, they clustered on the split-rail fence and shot across the patio and taunted me with their furry little tails held high. They nibbled on my dormant tulip bulbs and honeycombed the spaces between the stones outside my kitchen window with tunnels.

The local woodchucks, hearing of the burrowing possibilities, gathered in colonies on the old barn site. Here they designed several back doors, front doors, and side doors that showed up overnight in the yard, under cover of the myrtle patch in front of the pole barn, and finally, as the last insult, on opposite sides of Wayne's studio, a small building in the side yard. They mounded the dirt and left a neat tunnel that disappeared under the wooden floor on one side and reappeared with a matching pile of dirt on the other side.

Now woodchucks are usually quite innocuous creatures that tend to sit up on their furry little backsides watching the world pass by, their large, yellow buck teeth showing in a kind of engaging grin. Not this colony. Wary and easily spooked, they shot for the brush pile beyond the lawn at the first movement of humans, and they would have hardly been noticed had it not been for the mounds of dirt surrounding their entrances, or the abrupt shock of stepping into an exit hole hidden beneath ground cover.

I dragged out the live trap and baited it with marshmallows which disappeared in the night, the trap door sprung and tightly closed, but nothing inside. Cantaloupe likewise was devoured and the trap door closed, with no woodchuck trapped inside. In desperation I sprinkled cayenne pepper around the burrows and poured a quart of ammonia into the tunnel under the studio. No effect. The mound of dirt grew larger and the pepper disappeared underneath the pile.

As a last resort I dusted off the double-barrel 20 gauge and leaned it in the corner by the back door, ready to blast away at the first sight of a woodchuck emerging from under the building. To date the gun remains unfired, the word apparently having gotten out that the homeowner was hopping mad and armed. No sign of the woodchucks in days.

Overshadowing all of this drama was the theater of war pitting me against raccoons. This kept me up at night and caused my eyes to narrow to wicked little slits of malevolence. They were out there, under cover of night, nosing about, tipping things over, digging in the flower pots, ravaging and overturning anything that might be concealing food.

First they turned their attention to the bird feeder. Climbing the sycamore tree, they inched their way down a spindly branch to the wooden feeder. Their deft little paws unhooked the lid, and they ate the seeds. They left the feeder hanging askew, the lid dangling from a broken hinge.

The hummingbird feeder was next. They climbed the tall square post that held my purple clematis, moved along the cross arm above, and managed to unhook the glass feeder and drop it to the ground below. They broke the attached plastic base that held the nectar ports and left everything covered in sticky paw prints.

The next night they discovered the grape jelly feeder that I had forgotten to bring in at dusk. It hung opposite the hummingbird feeder and was securely attached by a metal hook. They cleverly figured out how to tilt the container and devour the jelly, all the while hanging seven feet above the ground.

The following morning I collected the feeder, scrubbed away their paw prints, refilled it and hung it back on the crossbar outside my kitchen window. That night they repeated their raid, this time detaching the feeder from the post and leaving it empty in the dirt below.

The third night, having refilled the feeder and foolishly left it outside after dark, I awoke to the realization of my carelessness. Too late to do anything about it now, I thought. Maybe they went elsewhere for nocturnal noshing. Not so. Having developed a taste for sweets, they detached the feeder from the hook and, apparently tucking it under a front paw, ran off with the entire thing. No trace, no plastic left behind - gone. We never did find where they had taken it. The wretched little marauders could now add grand theft to their list of sins.

What happened next is probably my fault, what with me dangling grape jelly from a post in my garden, and obligingly refilling it three nights running. I unwittingly fostered a taste for fruit in the hairy little raiders, and when the jelly connection dried up they turned to my raspberry patch.

I had been watching the patch for weeks, happily awaiting the day when I could begin picking the glorious red berries and turning them into jam for the winter ahead. There is something so satisfying about tending to a patch of berries. I had spent weeks late last fall thinning, weeding, and cutting back the canes to promote a heavy spring crop. And here they stood, loaded with lush fruit ripening under the June sun.

Then the raccoons moved in. On their deft little paws they wove among the canes, sniffing and nibbling, and finally, standing on their hind legs they dragged down clusters of fruit. Having no intention of sharing with the homeowner, they stripped the branches clean and left them dangling down, hanging by threads to wither in the next day's sunshine.

We tried every trick we could think of to stop the pillage. My live trap was obviously no match for such clever creatures, so I looked for other means to discourage them. The plastic owl perched on a shovel handle in the middle of the patch had been effective in repelling daytime robins, but nighttime thieves paid it no attention. We plugged a radio into an extension cord and turned up the volume at dusk, but music apparently stimulated their appetites, entertaining them while they ate.

We found an old electronic gadget that purportedly emitted a high-frequency sound that hurt the ears of small, hairy animals and sent them scurrying away with nagging headaches. We plugged it in and aimed the speaker at the berry patch. It was difficult to determine if these measures worked, most of the berries having been eaten already, and a new buffet opening just a few dozen yards to the south - my early transparent apple tree that was ripening and beginning to drop a few apples to the lawn below.

And that is where they are tonight - out in the dark with their pointed noses and sharp little teeth crunching on wind-falls, making little snuffling noises as they eye the tree and estimate how long the fallen apples will last and when it will be necessary to climb the tree for more. Then they will scrabble up the tree and crawl out on slender branches, breaking them or leaving them to dangle at crazy angles while the raccoons detach the apples and drop them to the grass below.

All this happens under cover of darkness. At the first streaks of dawn in the eastern sky they will amble toward the cornfield at the edge of the lawn and disappear into the green forest of cornstalks. They will head back to the woods beyond to climb trees and spend the upcoming day slumbering until the next sunset.

How they rile my homeowner's heart! I would gladly share my bounty with the creatures of nature, but I expect fair play in return. Not only do the raccoons plunder and devour their share, they take mine, leaving broken branches as well as broken dreams behind. They come under cover of darkness, spend the night gorging on my produce while I sleep in innocent bliss, then scuttle away at the crack of dawn leaving me to shake my fist in impotent anger at the desolation they have left behind.

I think the real issue here goes beyond a few quarts of raspberries. I think I am really annoyed with them because I am bigger and smarter and own the land and do the work and they saunter in, reap the harvest, and leave piles of seedy droppings behind to remind me that I have been had and they have won.

How I hate raccoons!

CHAPTER 16

WINTER MUSINGS

Winter hit hard and fast this year. One day I was hoeing crab grass in the blueberry patch and the next I was bent double struggling through wind-whipped snow in search of the scoop shovel.

A fluke, I thought, summer will return, or at least the charm of Michigan autumn. Not so. The weather knuckled down and got serious. Snow fell, drifted in undulating waves, and stayed for the duration. The sun sulked behind clouds, peering out in rare and brief intervals, and then feebly withdrawing above the next Arctic blast.

Leaves rattled in the wind, frozen to their summer branches before they could fall in autumnal heaps. The yard became a white palate with bits of vegetation embedded in the frozen crust beneath the trees. The wind blew relentlessly and bitterly from the north, blistering our summer skin with cold.

The year pitched and skidded toward Christmas. At least it will be white, we bravely declared, trying to comfort ourselves.

The weekend before Christmas white changed to crystalline. Rain fell heavily, coating our world with a growing shell of ice. Branches bowed under the weight, creaked and split to hang from raw wounds or to plummet to the ground and freeze grotesquely in the lake below. The night became a series of quiet moments punctuated by cannon-like cracks as heavy branches crashed down onto the roof and porch.

Then in a final exertion of nature's cold dominion, the lights flickered and went out. The house became a tomb of eerie silence. Why didn't we fill water buckets, we asked ourselves. Where are the candles? Do we have any matches?

When we finally found a candle and lit it, we stood in its tiny ring of light and contemplated our fate. It was likely that power lines were down under the burden of ice, and, unlike brief summer outages, it might take hours or days to repair the damage and restore electricity.

There was nothing to do except huddle under a pile blankets on the bed and wait for daybreak.

Dawn revealed a world of stark and grotesque beauty. The pale sun on the ice-encrusted trees unleashed brilliant points of light, as it had rained diamonds in the night. The wind harried the branches and they moved stiffly under their cold glitter. The birch tree, a survivor of decades of storms, gave up one limb after another, and my heart broke with each ragged wound that emerged.

We became aware of our frailty very quickly; Mother Nature was a force to be reckoned with. We were reduced to weak creatures who were powerless to do anything except huddle under blankets and shiver. The house became a museum of useless artifacts. Appliances, faucets, lamps, computers, phones - all were ludicrous reminders of our reliance upon electricity to power them.

Then, miraculously, our son-in-law Kurt appeared at the back door with a small generator. He ran three extension cords through the back room window, fired up the generator, and we had a basement freezer running, a refrigerator which lit up when I opened the door, and an electric power strip in the living room to power a lamp and small space heater. We hung a quilt at the door and our living room became a fragile cocoon of scant comfort the next four days.

There we listened to the relentless wind and watched the frigid world outside as it swayed crazily in nature's onslaught. As days and nights blended into a slow-moving stream, we began to change. Our usual routine was shattered like the ice that rattled down on our roof from the ancient pine tree above. There was nothing to do but concentrate on the most elemental aspects of life - staying warm and eating.

Nearly all other activities became irrelevant or impossible. The rituals of cleaning ourselves and our surroundings gave way to a quick brushing of teeth and an occasional attempt to tidy our living room. The only job that was absolutely essential and around which our lives centered was fueling the generator with gasoline; every five hours meant adding layers for warmth, pushing through the drifts that piled against the back door, and filling the tank with the golden fluid that was nearly as important to our existence as the blood in our veins.

That rhythm - passing a few hours and then filling the gas tank - replaced our usual daytime - nighttime cycle. Twenty four hours changed from two halves into five-hour segments of eating, talking, and napping, but always watching the clock as it measured the time until the generator needed to be fueled.

Our world began to narrow inward in a surprisingly pleasant way. We began to listen to each other undistracted by the electronic humming and chirping and buzzing of a normal, electric house. The sounds became natural and rational; our voices, sleet hitting the windows, the creaking of an old house feeling the cold in its bones. The world beyond our icy acres faded away and we began to talk. We talked about things buried deep in our hearts and memories. We warmed ourselves with the blessings of the past -- our children and grandchildren, our long and pleasant marriage, the security of life in our beloved country, the comfort that God was with us in all circumstances.

Then in a brilliant instant we were thrust back into our old life. Lights blazed. The furnace whirred. Phones and TV's and computers crackled and snapped and reset themselves. For a moment we were bewildered by the abrupt change. Then, with joy tinged by regret, we rejoined our old world.

No more hours of quiet talking and hasty trips to a cold kitchen for a simple meal. Time to think of bill paying and laundry and cleaning and cooking. Time to begin shoveling snow and showering and calling friends and listening to the news of a chaotic world.

Everything, even a winter ice storm and power outage, has moments of blessings tucked away for those who seek them.

CHAPTER 17

MISPLACING CHILDREN AND
OTHER VALUABLES

My family has always been a bit lax about remembering where they have put things. I believe this all started with Mother. She had a pretty good grasp of the broader picture, such as how many children she had or whether summer was just beginning or ending, but specifics often times escaped her.

The question "Kids, have you seen my girdle?" still worms its way into my thoughts, like the words of an old song that get hold of you and won't let go. We were always aghast at the thoughts of accidentally touching Mother's girdle, let alone deliberately hiding it somewhere. It was clean, mind you, but not something you wanted to pick up and examine. Unlike today's lacy, sleek garments meant to peep out at cleavages or shape the derriere, girdles in the 1940's were serious instruments of containment made of industrial elastic from which dangled garters to grip one's nylon stockings with rubber nubbins. Mother's girdle looked strangely alive, shrinking away from you when you touched it like a sea creature accidentally stepped on at high tide. To keep the peace, we all knew that it was best to scurry around and look in drawers or behind the couch or under the bed until Mother and her girdle were reunited.

She was also careless with things like her favorite paring knife or her garden hoe. We were eyed suspiciously as being the probable culprits in the disappearance of these items, but protesting did little more than annoy her, so we kept our mouths shut and joined the search until the missing items showed up.

I am afraid I have inherited this tendency to misplace important things. I cannot fathom the hours I have spent looking for the instructions for assembling my rolling garden cart, or the receipt for a new kitchen gadget that stopped working prematurely. My glasses are never where I left them, and the keys to the car are just as problematic.

But I have seldom, if ever, lost something really important, like a grandchild. Not until the summer I took TK to the flea market in Trufant, that is.

Trufant was the mecca for oddities, relics of the past, and wondrous creations that stirred my collector's soul. I'd scour the rickety tables piled with the wares of venders who had cleaned out their basements and garages and barns. When I found something that caught my eye and arrived at a price that satisfied both me and the vender, into my duffel bag the treasure would go.

TK sometimes went with me to my favorite hunting grounds. He learned to spot bargains, and little by little he turned into a savvy shopper who pointed out things I had missed.

One day we decided to try our hand at selling at the flea market instead of just buying. So at dawn we parked the van, set up a few card tables, and piled our surplus on them and waited for the customers to roll in.

As the morning passed we sold a bit here and there, but our wares failed to disappear at the rate we had hoped for. TK grew a bit impatient and began to pace around and fidget. His dream of making a tidy profit from the sale of his baseball cards and hot wheels began to fade.

His interest began to shift from his own table to the tables of others whose wares were undoubtedly more appealing than the things we had brought. By this time the usual crowd had arrived and was clogging the aisles, hundreds of shoppers moving along like a languid river.

"Nana, is it all right if I go off and look for some fishing lures?" TK asked hopefully.

Call it negligence, or too much sun, or a temporary lapse of good judgment, but I said glibly, "Sure, TK. Just don't be gone too long." I said nothing more, no grandmotherly admonishments like "Stay within sight of our tables," or "Be back in five minutes," or "Scream bloody murder if any weird stranger lays a hand on you."

So off went my nine-year-old grandson, a mere slip of a boy, blond, beautiful, and totally unchaperoned. And I, his protector and guardian, was oblivious.

I sat behind the card table and nodded off in the warm mid-morning sun. An occasional shopper would pull me back into alertness, but I would quickly return to my pleasant state of drowsiness.

Suddenly I jerked to attention. Good grief, what had I done? I looked around for TK to no avail. I had sent my youngest grandson off to brush elbows with who knew what collection of degenerates and derelicts! He had been gone for hours, I thought, although my watch told me it had only been twenty minutes.

My maternal heart raced and I felt the cold rock in my stomach that every adult has felt when a child in her charge is missing and unaccounted for. I watched the people strolling down the shopping aisles, and they looked shifty and dangerous, their eyes darting about for, I was certain, small children to snatch and stuff in the trunks of their cars and high-tail it for the nearest big city to sell their catch to sinister foreign buyers.

What was I going to tell his parents, I wondered. They would disown me and I would forever be in deepest disgrace. This rather self-serving bit of shallow thinking only added to my misery.

I scanned the crowd for a glimpse of a slender boy in shorts and...good heavens, I thought. I don't even know how he was dressed. "What was your grandson wearing," the policeman would ask, and I would look idiotically blank and reply, "I didn't notice." What kind of nincompoop was I, anyway?

Five more minutes had passed, my watch told me. I decided I had to do something. Leaving my booth space I walked toward the center of the market where a sprawling old building stood shrouded in galvanized metal sheets and where, I hoped, I'd find someone in charge. I found only shoppers and vendors, all of which were looking increasingly suspicious and menacing.

At last I caught a glimpse of the manager riding down an aisle in his golf cart. I pursued him shouting, "Excuse me, sir, pardon me, could you please help me?" I could tell by his expression that he was not partial to harried grandmothers in full-blown crisis.

Reluctantly he stopped and waited for me to catch my breath and give him the sorry details.

"Do you have a public address system?" I gasped. "My grandson is somewhere on the grounds and I am getting worried. He should have been back at our booth long ago."

The manager sighed in resignation, turned off the motor of his cart, and swung his legs over the side. "What is his name?" he asked dully.

"TK," I said, my voice quavering. "Just ask him to please return to his Grandma's booth."

He disappeared behind a rusty door and minutes later I heard electronic crackling and popping as he turned up the volume.

Then over the speakers aimed in all four directions atop the office roof I heard in deafening tones, "TK, attention TK! Your Grandmother is worried sick and you need to get back to her booth right this minute! Attention, TK. Get back to your Grandma immediately. Return to your Grandma's booth this minute!"

My heart sank. My gentle grandson reacted to the least suggestion of criticism or correction by shrinking in embarrassment and humiliation. Not only had I scared the pants off him by sending an electronic message of doom, but it had been delivered by a stranger with a deep voice who bellowed over the loud speaker like an enraged bull. I'm sorry, TK, I breathed inwardly. I didn't mean to subject you to public scorn.

I returned to my booth and waited. A few minutes later I spied my grandson walking rapidly toward me, eyes wild and face ashen. He tried to explain where he had been and how he got involved in a discussion with a fishing lure vendor and didn't realize he'd been gone so long. I should just have murmured something vague and let it drop, but I felt the need to apologize and explain and justify my paranoid behavior. My brain told my mouth to close tightly and say no more, but my emotions overruled and I just kept blathering.

Tears welled up in TK's eyes and he shrank away from me and fled to the van where he sat crouched over and spilling abject misery. It was too late to make things better. I had embarrassed him and wounded his spirit to the depths. I could do nothing but wait it out. There we sat, a child in retreat holed up in the van, and a grandmother sitting outside, face frozen in a plastic pose and heart mirroring her grandson's pain.

Eventually the morning passed and it was time to leave. The flurry of activity packing up our unsold merchandise diverted us, and we talked about trivial things with artificial enthusiasm. Halfway home I presented a peace offering of an enormous burger served with fries and a Mountain Dew, delivered by a waiter who assumed we were having a pleasant lunch out and chatted with breezy nonchalance. That helped.

By the time we reached TK's home we were nearly back to normal. But the ground we had just covered was still too painful to revisit. I knew better than to reopen the wound by adding a final apology. So waving goodbye and smiling as I left him at his back door would have to do.

Some day in the far-away future a grown-up TK will probably temporarily misplace something of great value, like a child left in his keeping. Then he will look back on that fateful day at the Trufant flea market and say with pathos, "Aw, Nana, now I understand."

ABOUT THE AUTHOR

Polly Rogers Brown is a retired high school English teacher. Ever enjoying a good story, she has taken delight in recounting to her seven grandchildren some of her favorite memories—both warmly amusing and instructional—from her 1940s childhood experiences of life and family.

These regular retellings inspired her to write *Who Dyed My Hair White in the Night? Reflections of a Perennial Child,* an account of her colorful and fascinating life in a rural farm town in lower Michigan.

Made in the USA
Lexington, KY
17 February 2017